# ALFRED SCHNITTKE'S CONCERTO GROSSO NO. 1

*Oxford* KEYNOTES
*Series Editor*   KEVIN C. KARNES

# ALFRED SCHNITTKE'S Concerto Grosso No. 1

PETER J. SCHMELZ

OXFORD
UNIVERSITY PRESS

Oxford University Press is a department of the University of Oxford. It furthers
the University's objective of excellence in research, scholarship, and education
by publishing worldwide. Oxford is a registered trade mark of Oxford University
Press in the UK and certain other countries.

Published in the United States of America by Oxford University Press
198 Madison Avenue, New York, NY 10016, United States of America.

Library of Congress Cataloging-in-Publication Data
Names: Schmelz, Peter John, author. | Schnittke, Alfred, 1934–1998. Concerti
grossi, no. 1.
Title: Alfred Schnittke's Concerto grosso no. 1 / Peter J. Schmelz.
Description: New York, NY : Oxford University Press, [2019] | Series: Oxford
keynotes | Includes bibliographical references and index.
Identifiers: LCCN 2018048156 | ISBN 9780190653712 (hardcover : alk. paper) |
ISBN 9780190653729 (pbk. : alk. paper)
Classification: LCC ML410.S276 S3 2019 | DDC 784.2/3—dc23
LC record available at https://lccn.loc.gov/2018048156

9 8 7 6 5 4 3 2 1

Paperback printed by Webcom, Inc., Canada
Hardback printed by Bridgeport National Bindery, Inc., United States of America

# Series Editor's
# INTRODUCTION

Oxford Keynotes reimagines the canons of Western music for the twenty-first century. With each of its volumes dedicated to a single composition or album, the series provides an informed, critical, and provocative companion to music as artwork and experience. Books in the series explore how works of music have engaged listeners, performers, artists, and others through history and in the present. They illuminate the roles of musicians and musics in shaping Western cultures and societies, and they seek to spark discussion of ongoing transitions in contemporary musical landscapes. Each approaches its key work in a unique way, tailored to the distinct opportunities that the work presents. Targeted at performers, curious listeners, and advanced undergraduates, volumes in the series are written by expert and engaging voices in their fields, and will therefore be of significant interest to scholars and critics as well.

In selecting titles for the series, Oxford Keynotes balances two ways of defining the canons of Western music: as lists of works that critics and scholars deem to have articulated key moments in the history of the art, and as lists of works that comprise the bulk of what consumers listen to, purchase, and perform today. Often, the two lists intersect, but the overlap is imperfect. While not neglecting the first, Oxford Keynotes gives considerable weight to the second. It confronts the musicological canon with the living repertoire of performance and recording in classical, popular, jazz, and other idioms. And it seeks to expand that living repertoire through the latest musicological research.

Kevin C. Karnes
Emory University

# CONTENTS

# ABOUT THE
# COMPANION WEBSITE

O XFORD HAS CREATED A website to accompany *Alfred Schnittke's Concerto Grosso No. 1*. Material that cannot be made available in a book is provided here, including rare recordings and video clips as well as color versions of many of the figures. Readers are encouraged to consult this resource while reading the book. Examples available online are indicated in the text with Oxford's symbol ⊙.

http://www.oup.com/us/ascgn1
Username: Music3
Password: Book3234

The reader is invited to explore the full catalogue of Oxford Keynotes volumes on the series homepage.
www.oup.com/us/oxfordkeynotes

# ACKNOWLEDGMENTS

I AM GRATEFUL TO many individuals and institutions for assistance in preparing this volume. First, I would like to thank everyone at the American Academy in Berlin for their support and encouragement as I was finishing the manuscript. I would especially like to single out Michael Steinberg, Carol Scherer, René Ahlborn, Yolande Korb, and Kelly Pocklington, as well as my fellow fellows: Nancy Foner, Sugi Ganeshananthan, Dilip Gaonkar, Aglaya Glebova, Kati Marton, Jacqueline E. Ross, Özge Samanci, A. L. Steiner, Kira Thurman, and Thomas Chatterton Williams.

I also would like to thank Heather Landes, director of the School of Music at Arizona State University, Tempe, for her encouragement and help, as well as my colleagues in the musicology area and the staff of the School of Music, especially Adrienne Goglia, Lori Pollock, and Nancy Sell. I am also beholden to the hardworking staff of the Music Library and Interlibrary Loan at ASU, especially Linda Elsasser, Christopher Mehrens, and Jeffrey Norman.

For specific assistance with my research for this book, I am grateful to Elena and Sergey Dubinets, Oleh Krysa,

Aleksey Lyubimov, Svetlana Savenko, and Jonathan Yaeger, as well as Lesley Ruthven and Jack Mulvaney at Special Collections and Archives, Goldsmiths, University of London; Mary Larkin at the Harris Theater for Music and Dance in Chicago; Katerina Kordatou at the Hamburg Ballett John Neumeier; Christine Henninger and the other staff members at the MIME Centrum Berlin (Internationales Theaterinstitut Zentrum Deutschland); the very helpful archivists at the Akademie der Künste in Berlin; and the staff and archivists at the Paul Sacher Stiftung in Basel, particularly Felix Meyer, Heidy Zimmermann, and Matthias Kassel. I am thankful to WDR for supplying me with a copy of the 1977 television broadcast of the Concerto Grosso no. 1. I also wish to acknowledge Vladimir Padunov and the University of Pittsburgh Slavic and East European Film Collection, where I first watched several of the films cited in this book a decade ago, before they became widely available on the Internet or through other commercial channels. Donna Wilson quickly and effortlessly created my music examples. I offer my appreciation as well to Wendy Keebler for her careful, sensitive copyediting.

In addition to the names listed above, I owe many others for their advice, inspiration, and friendship, including (but by no means limited to) Andrea Bohlman, Pat Burke, Joy Calico, James Currie, Todd Decker, Ryan Dohoney, Eric Drott, Melina Esse, Pauline Fairclough, Danielle Fosler-Lussier, Marina Frolova-Walker, Mathew Gelbart, Lisa Jakelski, Keeril Makan, Olga Manulkina, Craig Monson, Klára Móricz, Simon Morrison, Inna Naroditskaya, Dolores Pesce, Bill Quillen, Wolfgang Rathert, Jesse Rodin, Phil Rupprecht, Anne Shreffler, Richard Taruskin, Joan

Titus, Miriam Tripaldi, John Turci-Escobar, Holly Watkins, Marianne Wheeldon, and Patrick Zuk.

I presented material from this project at conferences and talks at Louisiana State University, the Eastman School of Music, and the 2017 International Musicological Society Congress in Tokyo. I thank the organizers at all of these events as well as the audiences for their many perceptive questions.

This book would not have happened if the incomparable Kevin Karnes had not suggested it; and Suzanne Ryan was an ideal editor, calm, clearheaded, and emboldening. I owe them both a great deal.

Julian, Elia, and Alexander, as always, helped in ways too varied and numerous to list.

I dedicate this book to my father, who unwittingly set all of this in motion many years ago by mentioning the name Shostakovich.

# ARCHIVES AND
# SOURCES

ADK             Archiv der Akademie der Künste, Berlin
                (with the collection identified in each
                citation).

*Besedy*          *Besedy s Al'fredom Shnitke*, ed. Aleksandr
                Ivashkin (1st ed. Moscow: RIK "Kul'tura,"
                1994; 2nd ed. Moscow: Klassika-XXI, 2005).

*Critical Edition* Alfred Schnittke, *Concerto Grosso No. 1 dlia
                dvukh skripok (ili fleity i goboia), klavesina,
                fortepiano i strunnogo orkestra, Critical
                Edition, Based on the Composer's Archival
                Materials*, ed. Aleksei Vul'fson and Elena
                Isaenko, Collected Works, series III, vol.
                20 (Saint Petersburg: Kompozitor, 2013).

Festschrift     *Alfred Schnittke zum 60 Geburtstag*, ed.
                Jürgen Köchel, Hans-Ulrich Duffek, Helmut
                Peters, et al. (Hamburg: Sikorski, 1994).

*Gody*            *Gody neizvestnosti Al'freda Shnitke*, ed.
                Dmitrii Shul'gin (1st ed. Moscow: Delovaia
                Liga, 1993; rev. ed. Direkt-Media, 2014; all
                references are to 1993 ed.).

| | |
|---|---|
| Kholopova | Valentina Kholopova, *Kompozitor Al'fred Shnitke* (1st ed. Chelyabinsk: Arkaim, 2003; 2nd ed. Moscow: Kompozitor, 2008; all references are to 2008 ed.). |
| *Posviashchaetsia* | *Al'fredu Shnitke posviashchaetsia* (Moscow: Kompozitor; volume number and date of publication are specified in each citation). |
| *Reader* | *A Schnittke Reader*, ed. Alexander Ivashkin (Bloomington and Indianapolis: Indiana University Press, 2002). |
| SCG | Schnittke Collection, Goldsmiths, University of London. |
| *Stat'i* | Al'fred Shnitke, *Stat'i o muzyke* (Moscow: Kompozitor, 2004). |
| Universal | Alfred Schnittke, *Concerto Grosso* [no. 1] (Vienna: Universal Edition, 1978). |

# ALFRED SCHNITTKE'S CONCERTO GROSSO NO. 1

## CHAPTER 1

# PRELUDIO

A TOLLING MELODY. UNIDENTIFIABLE, DISTANT, funereal. Simple, it circles upon itself. Familiar. Foreign. Over before starting, it fades to black. A violin enters, its partner repeats: slow, tentative. Nearly static, they stay on two notes yet slowly build. Another, older instrument, a harpsichord, buttresses faintly the struggling melody. The violins ache higher, reaching anguished peaks above sighing strings. The harpsichord tests isolated notes, uncertain. Cautious, chanting melodies crawl forth, louder, straining against ghostly counterpoint from the soloists. Another peak—the duo in tandem repeat melodies in crunching embrace. The ensemble acquiesces. Barely perceptible, it, like the opening incantation, fades. Inexorable. Stuck (▶ audio 1.1).

# I

The prelude to Alfred Schnittke's Concerto Grosso no. 1 sets forth the composition in condensed form. It introduces all the participants, prepares all the conflicts. The opening evocation captures the otherworldliness of the whole. It puts in motion oscillations between popular and serious, foreground and background, intelligibility and opacity, dream and reality, irony and earnestness, and hope and despair that drive the entire work—a number of paradoxes with no clear answers. This ambiguous, chorale-like opening—church or folk, sacrament or sacrilege?—is doubly estranged by the means of its production: a prepared piano, an unlikely appearance by American composer John Cage's innovative alteration of the piano's sound by inserting foreign materials, screws, washers, or, in this case, kopeks.[1] The two soloists form a tight, harmoniously discordant pair. The ensemble provides a hushed backdrop. The harpsichord is a witless bystander called to be an unlikely participant.

All of this requires explanation, to which the remainder of this book is dedicated. Listening closely, guided by the composition, we will take account of the genesis, construction, first performances, and critical and public impact of this most unusual of compositions—both throwback and view forward. Time is its linchpin. Its agglomeration of styles guides yet confuses. Responding to a recent profile of American rock musician Jack White, an admirer commented: "White's polymorphous musical style—from McCartney-esque ballads to giant rock anthems and wailing blues homages—is refreshing for so many listeners because he isn't just mining the musical canon; he's writing new songs out of the past."[2] In his Concerto Grosso no. 1,

Schnittke did something similar. With its backward glances, he attempted, however belatedly and foolhardily, to compose the present. No wonder that for those in the Soviet Union and eager foreign listeners alike, it became a sonic marker of glasnost and perestroika, of Russianness and Sovietness at the end of the Cold War. The Concerto Grosso no. 1 raised larger questions—it became a Rorschach test for contemporary anxieties about freedom and control, the tortured past and the uncertain future.

Much of the composition's weirdness and its emotional impact can be credited to the personality and occupations of its creator. A critic once called Schnittke "the Russian with the German name," as good an encapsulation as any of his inherent dividedness, and his inherent foreignness, both to himself and to others.[3] Born in 1934 to a Jewish father and a German mother in the Volga-German settlement of Engels in the Soviet Union, Schnittke near the end of his life often emphasized that he possessed "not a single drop of Russian blood."[4] His dividedness could cause him anguish; it caused others confusion. What was he? Some Russians were "troubled by the foreign-sounding name Schnittke." They wondered "whether he is 'one of ours.'"[5]

Schnittke's life in the Soviet Union was riddled with contradictions: he was supported and encouraged yet thwarted, recognized as troubling yet important by both advocates and opponents. Drawn to music from an early age, he, like many Soviet composers from his generation, pushed against the constraints of his official, conservative musical education. By the late 1950s, nearing graduation, he landed on a topic of considerable political importance: the American bombing of Nagasaki near the end of

World War II. He wrote a cantata setting texts by Japanese poets describing the bombing and its tragic aftermath. It was sure to be a hit because it checked all the socialist-realist boxes: accessibility, relevance, and proper "idea content." It allowed for an advantageous comparison of the peace-loving Soviets and the warmongering Americans. But Schnittke's curiosity and his penchant for experimentation caused things to hit a snag. He depicted the atom-bomb blast a bit too creatively—aiming to represent the unrepresentable, he turned for a model to the noisiest, most apocalyptic music he could imagine: Igor Stravinsky's *The Rite of Spring*. But Stravinsky was still persona non grata in the Soviet Union, and Schnittke's academic committee forced him to try again. He ultimately passed, and the experience did not dissuade him from his musical experiments.[6]

Instead, over the course of the 1960s, Schnittke, an intense, analytical thinker, dove into the compositional intricacies of twelve-tone composition and serialism, then highly fashionable in Western Europe and America and as a result very attractive to young, curious composers in the Soviet Union. Schnittke tried one approach, then another, blending serial techniques with other contemporary approaches, chief among them aleatory—or quasi-improvisational—devices. In his *Music for Chamber Orchestra* (1964), he went the farthest he ever would, applying serial techniques to its melody, the durations of each pitch in the melody, and the number of pitches in each of its subsections.[7] But he began to feel constrained.

His next compositions were both serial and programmatic. The programs justified what Schnittke had started to feel was an arbitrary system. He thought in musical pictures and sonic dramas, however much he, like many composers, later vacillated about the existence or necessity of programs for understanding his compositions.[8] His Second Violin Concerto (1966) was based on Christ's Passion, and his *Pianissimo* for orchestra (1968), his last exclusively serial composition, was a setting of Franz Kafka's terrifying short story "In the Penal Colony"; Schnittke represented the repetitive punishment of the criminal with repeated twelve-tone rows.[9]

Schnittke clearly felt pained; serialism had become torture. Change was needed but slow to emerge. The trouble lay in Schnittke's precarious professional situation. Because his music pushed boundaries and broke official taboos, he had a difficult time earning a living as a composer of "serious" music. The Ministry of Culture refused to purchase his scores and paid very little when it did. He had trouble securing performances. But outlets existed: film, cartoons, television, and theater. Schnittke became an in-demand composer for mixed media of every sort.

Schnittke's extreme fluency in composing was a great asset. His surviving film scores show page after page of melodic invention, dreamed up quickly and rarely used in their entirety. The life of a film composer proved humbling, for he was required to subordinate his aesthetic goals to those of the director.[10] But film composition was also a boon. Schnittke had an orchestra at his beck and call, willing and ready to perform whatever unconventional tunes or outlandish sound effects he had imagined. And Soviet cartoons offered many justifications for outlandish sounds.[11]

Schnittke constantly tacked back and forth about his work for hire, as he did about so many things: whether he liked popular music or not, whether he composed voluntarily or involuntarily, the relationship between good and evil, reality and unreality. An interviewer later said that his favorite word was "yet . . . ."[12] But the back and forth between his day job and his real love, composing "serious" music, became too much. Rather than resolving antitheses, Schnittke practiced a more personal, less certain dialectic than the officially endorsed dialectical materialism of Soviet communism. He tried to allow antitheses to productively interact. He shaped a system that would incorporate both sides, all sides. He called it polystylism.

In a brief, influential essay titled "Polystylistic Tendencies of Contemporary Music," first presented publicly in 1971, Schnittke addressed the main points of his approach. It would capture the complexity of the contemporary soundscape: "It widens the range of expressive possibilities, it allows for the integration of 'low' and 'high' styles, of the 'banal' and the 'recherché'—that is, it creates a wider musical world and a general democratization of style."[13] Not long after he completed the Concerto Grosso no. 1, Schnittke noted the sounds that greeted him when he returned home: neighbors listening to loud music or playing their televisions at an excessive volume, people a floor below having a loud conversation. He narrated the noises of a large, congested city, amplified by technology. Rather than complaining or putting in earplugs, Schnittke adapted, turning vice into virtue: "And therefore it seems to me that perhaps my job is to record this entire stylistic kaleidoscope in order to reflect some of our reality."[14] He decided to document the chaos. Polystylism was his medium (figure 1.1).

FIGURE 1.1    Alfred Schnittke in the late 1960s or early 1970s. Photo ©
Marianna Volkov/Bridgeman Images. Used with permission.

Schnittke began having these thoughts in the late 1960s
and early 1970s as he was working on the music for an am-
bitious survey of twentieth-century history by film director
Mikhail Romm. Romm had made a name for himself with
documentaries—chief among them his film about the hor-
rors of the Third Reich, *Everyday Fascism* (*Obyknovennyi
fashizm*, 1966). Now at the end of his life, Romm took account of the major trends and upheavals of the past sev-
enty years worldwide. Schnittke was asked to write music
reflecting these upheavals, and to watch representative
footage from the film as he did so, scenes of protest, conflict, human tragedy, human striving, revolutions, two
world wars, and technological triumph and tragedy. The

experience touched him deeply. Schnittke resolved to write a composition that would similarly document contemporary reality. This became his Symphony no. 1.

In the symphony, which he completed in 1972, Schnittke included countless quotations—from Pyotr Tchaikovsky, Ludwig van Beethoven, Edvard Grieg, and Frédéric Chopin, among many others. He also inserted at the premiere an actual jazz ensemble, Moscow's renowned Melodiya group, along with raucous marches, preexisting and of his own invention. (In a sketch, he also toyed with using a rock group.)[15] The second movement included a pastiche of an eighteenth-century melody, a theme that Schnittke had first written as part of his score for a film with the marvelous name *Adventures of a Dentist* (*Pokhozhdenie zubnogo vracha*, dir. Elem Klimov, 1965) (► video 1.1). (This theme later became the second-movement Ballet of his 1972 *Suite in the Old Style*.) The last movement of the symphony included quotations from the Dies Irae funeral chant and a concatenation of funeral marches, an effect inspired by attending the burial of a friend's father and hearing competing funeral cortèges resound from opposite ends of the cemetery.

The composition was chaotic, lengthy, and loud. At its start, the musicians took the stage one by one, improvising. Schnittke wanted the effect to be the opposite of Joseph Haydn's *Farewell Symphony*, with musicians entering rather than exiting. The brass and woodwind players left the stage at the end of the second movement and returned at the beginning of the fourth movement.

Its first audience in February 1974 was astonished, even overwhelmed. They had never heard anything like it. Schnittke drew upon Charles Ives and Gustav Mahler as well as more recent European music, including Bernd Alois Zimmermann's opera *Die Soldaten* (premiered 1965), Henri Pousseur's opera *Votre Faust* (1960–68), and Luciano Berio's *Sinfonia* (1968–69), about which he had much to say in his polystylism lecture and in a subsequent analytical essay.[16] But few of his first listeners had heard those composers or those compositions. Soviet society had been slowly thawing over the past decade or so, but change was slow and incremental. There were many temporary or partial refreezes. Schnittke's symphony almost went unheard. He had to appeal to a colleague, Rodion Shchedrin, then chair of the Union of Composers of the Russian SFSR, for the go-ahead. But it could not be performed in Moscow. Schnittke and his supporters had to venture to the closed city of Gorky (now Nizhny Novgorod). Many made the pilgrimage. Others were able to hear the performance only on a widely circulated bootleg recording. (Although it has never officially been released, copies are still being passed around today.) Through its lo-fi haze, the excitement and energy are still palpable.

Later that year, the leading Soviet scholarly music periodical, *Sovetskaia muzyka*, devoted many pages to a transcript of a heated discussion of the symphony; several musicologists, theorists, and composers weighed in on its merits and defects. Many of these official listeners found it too chaotic and formless. Its "content"—a ubiquitous Soviet theoretical (i.e., socialist-realist) concept—was too ambiguous. Composer and musicologist Alexander Kurchenko complained that Schnittke had not provided the listener with enough guidance for judging the mishmash of styles.[17]

Yet even Kurchenko admitted Schnittke's "talent, erudition, and technical mastery."[18]

Where could he go next? How could Schnittke build upon a symphony that had included everything? As it often does, life unexpectedly intervened. Schnittke's mother died in 1972 of a stroke, and he immediately set to work writing a composition in her memory. It took him much effort and several false starts. The ultimate result was his Piano Quintet (1972–76), a work central to understanding the Concerto Grosso no. 1. Over the late 1960s, Schnittke had latched onto narratives, but his music remained fractured. Now he attempted to heal.

The quintet foregrounds a waltz and J. S. Bach's initials (B–A–C–H, or, in musical notes, B♭–A–C–B♮). But it lacks most of the polystylistic gestures that had so distinguished the symphony. Befitting its purpose, it was quieter and more intimate. Made up of five movements, it opens with foreboding; its language is weakly acidic. The piano plays a solemn chordal injunction, followed by tight echoing motion between the strings—sliding, dissonant scales similar to those in the Preludio of Concerto Grosso no. 1. The second movement is a hazy waltz heard through shimmering time, warped as with desert heat yet ice-cold. Slowly, it begins to burn, becoming more frantic near its end.

The quintet presents a strange, reduced polystylism. Schnittke's earlier Violin Sonata no. 2, "Quasi una sonata" ("Like a sonata"), for only two instruments (1968), sounded more forceful. The waltz is the sole other preexisting style sampled in the quintet. It returns in the final, fifth movement alongside a reference to BACH in violin 1 (mm. 79–80, not the first BACH motive in the quintet)

(▶ audio 1.2). But repetition continues to propel (if not stall) the work. A lovely melody arching high in the piano's right hand continues, heedless of the soft, vibratoless waltz in the other strings. Schnittke pushed extreme foreground and background effects, distilling the layers he set in extreme motion in his Symphony no. 1 and that he would continue using in the Concerto Grosso no. 1. The quintet's ending returns to the theatricality from earlier in the composition: the final melodic gesture in the piano in measures 194–98 is meant to be a silent echo, "without sound, almost only key noise."

The Piano Quintet's minimal means convey a nearly inert state of grief. Listeners such as young Soviet avant-garde composers Elena Firsova and Dmitri Smirnov abandoned Schnittke after hearing it, feeling that he had retreated too far from his earlier, more daring scores. He had returned to a "populist path" that resembled too closely "the style and means of classical Soviet music."[19]

Although Firsova and Smirnov did not make the connection, the "classical Soviet music" that Schnittke's quintet most resembled was Dmitri Shostakovich's, particularly Shostakovich's late compositions, among them his final string quartets. Schnittke's music (like Shostakovich's) now paradoxically contained both too few and too many meanings and subtexts. Despite the sparseness of the quintet, it felt overloaded. He did not intend for it to be dedicated to the recently deceased Shostakovich, although he admitted the possibility of "some resemblance in the general musical mood."[20] (Schnittke said that he had found only a single reference to Shostakovich's DSCH monogram, or D–E♭–C–B♮, in the quintet.) The resemblance had been much more explicit in Schnittke's contemporaneous *Prelude in Memory of Shostakovich* for two violins or one violin and tape (1975).[21]

As the Piano Quintet suggests, the music Schnittke wrote between his Symphony no. 1 and Concerto Grosso no. 1 expressed a more restrained polystylism. A few other compositions from this period are worth mentioning, one large-scale and several small-scale. Schnittke called his Requiem (1975) a "departure" from his quintet.[22] It continued the extroversive, capacious impulses from the Symphony no. 1 in a tamer guise. Certain moments swerve in the direction of popular music—the Credo in particular embraces a type of mid-1970s theatrical rock resembling Andrew Lloyd Webber's *Jesus Christ Superstar* (1970), then being widely passed around in the Soviet Union. (Schnittke heard it at this time.)[23]

The *Hymns* that Schnittke composed in the mid-1970s also point to general stylistic aspects of his Concerto Grosso no. 1. Only three of the four *Hymns* were composed before the Concerto Grosso: no. 1 for cello, harp, and timpani (1974), no. 2 for cello and double bass (1974), and no. 3 for cello, bassoon, harpsichord, and bells (1975). (*Hymn* no. 4 dates from 1979.)[24] These earnest compositions are pervaded with ritual and stillness. They expand a sense of hovering timelessness rarely found in earlier Schnittke. Nonetheless, a typical Schnittke obsessiveness reappears in *Hymn* no. 3, amplified by its odd ensemble. Originally scored for children's choir and bells and written for director Igor Talankin's film *Daytime Stars* (*Dnevnye zvezdy*,

1966), it was based on Schnittke's creative reimagining of old Russian chant. It presented an archaic polystylism (▶ video 1.2).[25]

Other works from around the time of Concerto Grosso no. 1 continued the overabundant exuberance of Schnittke's music from the late 1960s and early 1970s, among them his controversial, updated cadenzas to Beethoven's Violin Concerto. In his cadenza for the first movement, written in 1975 for violinist Mark Lubotsky, Schnittke accumulated excerpts from a number of famous violin concertos that shared a motivic resemblance to Beethoven's concerto: by Shostakovich, Béla Bartók, and Alban Berg (and also Bach, via Berg's concerto). He worked to integrate the quotations thematically, although it demanded "hellish effort" to do so.[26] He called it "building a house without nails"—he wanted it to be organic, seamless. The intent was serious and representative of Schnittke's overall compositional approach, which focused on structure and a clear motivation for uniting disparate elements. In 1977, Schnittke completed cadenzas for the other two movements of Beethoven's concerto; they were briefer and more gestural, less burdened by the signifying past.

In 1982, Gidon Kremer (b. 1947), a pivotal Schnittke advocate and one of the first performers of Concerto Grosso no. 1, whom we will discuss in greater detail later, recorded for Philips the Beethoven Violin Concerto with Schnittke's cadenzas accompanied by the Academy of St. Martin in the Fields conducted by Neville Marriner.[27] The cadenzas attracted a great deal of attention, much of it negative. Critics compared them to Marcel Duchamp drawing a mustache on the *Mona Lisa* in his *L.H.O.O.Q.* (1919).[28] But Schnittke held no Dada intent; the cadenzas were not meant to be absurd or facetious. He considered them a serious exercise in illuminating the complex shadow cast by Beethoven on the contemporary modernist canon. The dissonances are often jarring but never played for laughs. There is a clear message, particularly when Shostakovich's Violin Concerto forcefully emerges at the climax. As Kremer often explained, Beethoven's text gains a renewed vigor and a renewed grace from its encounter with the present (figure 1.2).[29]

Unlike the Beethoven cadenzas, two of Schnittke's other compositions from the mid- to late 1970s were intentionally humorous: *Moz-Art* (1976) and *Moz-Art à la Haydn* (1977).

FIGURE 1.2  Gidon Kremer in the 1970s. Photo © Suzie Maeder/Bridgeman Images. Used with permission.

He called *Moz-Art*, for two violins, "Most of all a musical joke, a humorous collage of Mozart's music."[30] Based on Mozart's unfinished Pantomime K. 416d, it included a grab bag of Mozart's greatest hits, with exaggerated effects, whistling, and grossly distended trills. The longer, larger *Moz-Art à la Haydn*, for two violin soloists and a string ensemble, followed the same principles and included much of the same material. The Haydnesque touch was an added theatrical element: musicians improvising at the start of the composition and exiting in the dark at its conclusion (as in his Symphony no. 1). The effect was not so much funny as strange. Critic and musicologist David Fanning wrote: "At times Schnittke seems to treat Mozart's material with the detached bemusement of a visitor from outer space confronting an artifact from a dead civilization—one that is evidently significant, but whose means of restoration have been lost in the sands of time."[31] Humor in Schnittke was always conditional and usually generated only nervous chuckles.[32] And as with so much of his music, the endings carried the greatest force. The somber close to *Moz-Art à la Haydn* casts suspicion on all that has gone before. The musicians exit in the dark as the conductor alone beats empty time.

**II**

It is a darkness from which the opening to Concerto Grosso no. 1 might plausibly emerge. Commentators have often reached for metaphors of broken machinery to summarize Schnittke's effects. Among the many alternative names Schnittke considered for *Moz-Art*, two stand out: "Prism of Time" (*Prizma vremeni*) and "Through the

Prism of Time, Shaking Off the Dust of the Ages" (*Cherez prismu vremeni, otriakhnuv pyl' vekov*).[33] A German critic reported two additional possibilities, perhaps mistranslations of these: "Clock of Dust" or the "Ravages of Time" (*Staubuhr* or *Der Zahn der Zeit*), suggesting a dissipating, dissolving timepiece, something conceived by Salvador Dalí.[34] The Concerto Grosso no. 1 was no different. Russian musicologist Svetlana Savenko writes that the "melancholy motive of the prepared piano that frames the Concerto Grosso no. 1 is a raspy [*okhripshaia*] music box from which everything appears in order to, at the very end, disappear back into it."[35] Musicologist Valentina Kholopova, using language nearly identical to Savenko's, said the theme is "literally the raspy [*khriplaia*] music of a clock" that Schnittke used "throughout the entire concerto grosso as a fatal refrain."[36] Like a mechanized version of Pandora's box, the prepared piano chorale releases, wheezing and sputtering, what we next hear. It foretells grim happenings (example 1.1).

At different moments, Schnittke called it a "lively children's chorale" and a "kind of sad children's song."[37] Neither description matches the original version of the music, which appeared at the very opening of the 1976 film *The Tale of the Moor of Peter the Great*, directed by Alexander Mitta after an unfinished novel by Alexander Pushkin. The chorale, scored for celesta with xylophone accompaniment, plays against the film's opening credits, illustrated by animated atavistic scenes from Russian folk tales and accompanied by ambient sounds—a rooster and bird calls. We see the rooster, workers reaping hay, a cat, fields, a man playing a flute for a dancing bear, a dark forest, and,

EXAMPLE 1.1  Alfred Schnittke, Concerto Grosso no. 1, opening measures, prepared piano chorale and violin soloists, measures 1–21.

finally, a firebird. The theme is cut off, and the credits continue over a new harpsichord melody (▶ video 1.3).

Schnittke originally intended the opening melody in the film to accompany the words from a New Year's carol (*koliadka*) for children's choir, an appeal to God beginning, "O man, your life is brief, sad, and pitiable, with fatal grief" (*O chelovek, nedolog tvoi vek, pechalen i smertnoiu skorb'iu zhalen*).[38] But this text—and its morose mood—did not make it into the film.[39] Listeners and performers such as violinist Oleh Krysa (b. 1942) were aware of the borrowing, recognizing that the prepared piano melody had originated in a film scored by Schnittke, but few, if any, remarked on the connection at the time (or later).[40]

The chorale thus traced a journey from a "lively," wordless, childlike song (with a gloomy submerged text) played by a celesta to an ominous refrain on a prepared piano. But that instrument had not been Schnittke's first choice; he originally had wanted a harpsichord to play the opening chorale and notated it this way in his first version of the concerto grosso. He altered it after the initial performances, presumably wanting a more mysterious, louder effect. The preparation of the piano by means of pieces of rubber or coins between each of the three strings in the treble-clef pitches is meant to produce "a dry, out-of-tune sound." Borrowing from the sustained reverberation of the chorale in the film, Schnittke indicated that the prepared piano should be "very highly amplified (especially in the fifth and sixth movement), so that the sound appears to fill the hall."[41]

The rendering of the opening chorale in performance is critical for the character of what follows. In Yuri Bashmet's

1988 recording, it is exceptionally clunky: broken machinery without any childlike innocence (see the appendix) ( audio 1.3). This recording amplifies the sense of stasis in the Preludio from the very first violin entrance; we have only just started and have already lost the path. Schnittke's own performances in a 1977 West German television broadcast and on the 1983 recording with Krysa and Georgian violinist Liana Isakadze (b. 1946) are more sensitive and more restrained (figure 1.3).

Krysa remarked, "everything is captured [*zakhvaten*] at the beginning of the composition"; it creates an "entire atmosphere" and sets the mood for what follows.[42] Several other motives and gestures presented in the Preludio

FIGURE 1.3   Liana Isakadze, cover of 1978 Melodiya LP of Ravel and Schnittke Violin Sonatas (detail) (33 S 10–10831-2).

appear throughout the Concerto Grosso no. 1. The initial entrance of the two violins after the prepared piano chorale resurfaces again and again. Its elements are simple, a small descent answered by a small rise, both rooted in dissonance. The first violin falls from E♭ to D; the second violin responds with an ascending second, seamlessly continuing the first violin D and rising back to E♭ (example 1.1; ▶ audio 1.4). As one violin rubs against the other, dissonances emerge; the closeness of the pitches raises uncomfortable vibrations in the ear and shudders on the skin. Schnittke offered his own reading of a similar gesture in György Ligeti's orchestral composition *Lontano* (1967): "The most characteristic motive, a falling minor second, is deprived of conventional expressive effect (the traditional motive of a 'sigh') by a return to the initial note, which neutralizes it (a 'sigh' is expressive; 'inhaling' and 'exhaling' are not)."[43] Schnittke's Concerto Grosso no. 1 amplifies the effect of agonized, motionless motion—of treading water, gasping for air.

Other main themes include the schmaltzy half-step ascent in solo violin 1 in measures 20–21 (E♭–E♮–F).[44] Another recurring motive is the harpsichord figuration from the center of the movement (mm. 30–31)—a stalling out—dropping and then ascending (by dissonant sevenths and ninths, E♭–D–C–D♭), repeated and then cut off (just the first two pitches are heard) (example 1.2; ▶ audio 1.5). This motive appears again in the violins near the end of the Preludio, elsewhere in the movement, and throughout the score as a whole. Other notable moments are the exhausted exhalation of strings at rehearsal 3 and the following chantlike melody in a throaty, low-register solo violin 1 at rehearsal 4

EXAMPLE 1.2   Alfred Schnittke, Concerto Grosso no. 1, Preludio, harpsichord figuration, measures 30–31.

(▶ audio 1.6). The language in the movement is highly gestural, and many of the gestures recur again and again. Recurrence itself becomes a theme. Many of the ideas in the composition are based on the idea of repetition, most apparent in the swifter movements: 2 (Toccata) and 5 (Rondo).

Formally, the Preludio can be divided into two sections of rising action split by the harpsichord sevenths and ninths in measures 30–31. During the second buildup, just after rehearsal 6, the more momentous (and more directed) of the two, the first phrase of the prepared piano theme reappears in the background, now in the harpsichord, buried beneath the soloists and strings, a return that is not a return (▶ audio 1.7).

## III

The Concerto Grosso no. 1 represents a key inflection point in Schnittke's output and perhaps in Western music history. There is a consensus, at least among Western authors, that Schnittke's output is postmodern, if only for the vague similarities between the "coexisting plurality of style" in his concept of polystylism and the "wider perspectives of post-modernism in music," as Kenneth Gloag puts it.[45] Gloag explains further: "Schnittke does not directly invoke post-modernism to describe his own music but he is using language, and composing music, that already relates to what we now understand as postmodernism."[46] As Gloag's interpretation suggests, the diagnosis of postmodernism in Schnittke, like many discussions of postmodernism—exhaustively theorized yet still frustratingly amorphous—often relies more on sense than on substance.

*Postmodernism* as a term did not enter Soviet critical or academic vocabulary until the late 1980s and did not enter Russian musicological discussions until the early 2000s.[47] Perhaps because during his lifetime the responses to Schnittke first in the Soviet Union and then in Russia were made without recourse to postmodernism, Russian musicologists today are reluctant to call him an unqualified postmodernist. It is anachronistic, implying foreign intervention and appropriation. In an overview of musical postmodernism, Savenko notes the prominence accorded to Schnittke in Western discussions of postmodernism because "for a long time polystylism was considered the most adequate fulfillment of the beloved postmodern idea of a decentralized, chaotic world."[48] Onto Schnittke's music Western writers projected their own concerns.

Savenko admits that Schnittke's approach resembles postmodernism but makes several important caveats. Drawing on work by Alexander Ivashkin, she underscores the specific nature of Schnittke's "pluralism," the particular cast he gives to his quoted material. Ivashkin presented the argument in more detail. "In Schnittke," he wrote, "even though you can hear tunes that were in theory written by Tchaikovsky, Chopin or Johann Strauss, it does not feel like music quoted from their scores. It comes crippled by accidents and battered by everyday life, by official funerals, weddings, TV clips. These fragments come from what Soviet people were used to hearing: songs, marches and dances, the singing of the drunk."[49] According to this reading, Schnittke does more than quote his musical material; he takes it from a specific context: the lived experience of Soviet reality that inextricably marks it, at least for those who shared that reality.

Savenko further argues that Schnittke's polystylism is set apart because of his focus on tightly unifying all of his quotations, as he does, she says, with the "leit-intonational connections"—the tight thematic web—in his Concerto Grosso no. 1.[50] (The idea of "intonations" is drawn from the work of Russian composer-theorist Boris Asafyev and relates to the semiotic interpretation of musical motives, figurations, and textures; it does not refer to the English-language connotations of intonation: tuning or being in tune.)[51] "The sharper the polystylistic contrasts," Savenko argues, "the more concerned [Schnittke] was with the problem of unity, with a unified structure—features not fully in keeping with the postmodern paradigm."[52] Both Savenko and Ivashkin pit Berio's *Sinfonia* and Schnittke's Symphony no. 1 against each other and find Berio's to be the clearer example of postmodernism.[53] (The overwhelming influence of Berio clearly provoked anxiety in both Schnittke and his supporters.) But the desire to keep Schnittke separate and special often ignores the evidence. Berio was also deeply concerned with unity in his *Sinfonia*, as demonstrated by the pervasive theme of water running through the Mahler movement and many of its quotations (e.g., Claude Debussy's *La mer*).[54]

We quickly reach an impasse, caught between portrayals of Schnittke as either exceptional or representative. Yet both arguments have merit when considered as categories of reception rather than aesthetics.[55] For a majority of listeners (both Soviet and Western), the theory with which Schnittke was first explained and evaluated was not post-modernism but polystylism, a separate idea with a separate tradition, much of it Russian in origin.[56] Savenko has called Schnittke's Concerto Grosso no. 1 the "purest" form of polystylism in his output.[57] And in 1988, eleven years after its premiere, German critic Jörg Polzin called the Concerto Grosso no. 1 "generally one of the most-performed works of new music. Concert, radio, and television performances as well as four recordings attest to the extraordinary aura of this work, really the splicing together of the by-products of various films, which substantiates Schnittke's fame as a polystylist."[58] With the Concerto Grosso no. 1, the local phenomena of polystylism achieved global reach, if not fame; in the process, Western critics and scholars gradually identified and claimed it as postmodern.

The Concerto Grosso no. 1 was a pinnacle for Schnittke in many senses. It was the first to establish his reputation in the West. And it has become a canonic, if not reper-toire, work, performed and recorded with some frequency (there are six recordings currently in print and at least eight available; see the appendix). The work's recordings and performances continued to grow after 1988, at which point the peak of Schnittke's fame was still a few years off. Although his celebrity has waned somewhat, a course that we will trace near the end of this book, the Concerto Grosso no. 1 has retained its canonic and repertoire status. As a critic once remarked, it has become a "paradigmatic, almost textbook" piece, and indeed it features in leading textbooks of Western art music.[59]

A textbook piece demands, if not a textbook, then a dedicated study. This book provides for the first time a compact yet comprehensive consideration of Alfred Schnittke's Concerto Grosso no. 1 (1977). In the chapters that follow, we move from composition and performance to reception. I build on previous research on the Concerto Grosso no. 1 but push in other directions, drawing on little-cited materials, including correspondence and especially commentary in Russian. The core of my approach is phenomenological and experiential. This book has its roots in slow, concentrated listening, repeatedly hearing the composition in different recordings and in different circumstances, keeping track of the moment-to-moment details as well as their larger-scale implications, and paying attention to what critics have heard while also attending to perhaps yet-unheard moments. I place the sounding of the music in contemporary recordings within the composition's multifaceted genealogy. Ideally, readers will check and confirm the observations I make with the many examples and audio clips on this book's companion website. Despite the apparent separability of movements, chief among them movements 2 and 5 (Toccata and Rondo), the composition builds from moment to moment, movement to movement, sketching out an ongoing process of growth, conflict, and decay. References return, altered, transforming their contexts and, in turn, being transformed.

# CHAPTER 2

## TOCCATA

THE PRELUDIO LEADS NOWHERE. Yet we arrive. The Toccata begins abruptly, in sudden motion. Off and running, one violin desperately pursues the other at an ever-increasing volume. The texture alternately thickens and clarifies, complicated by furious, swarming strings. The buzzing builds to a fever pitch until the basses call for order. Seven fortissimo repeated dissonances (a minor seventh E/D) initiate a mawkish melody built from the repetition— the two soloists in a too-sweet canon (rehearsal 6).

Imitation consumes the texture. Echoes ripple across the ensemble, punctuated by jagged outbursts from the two soloists. They follow successive buildups and fade-outs with a declaration: Triumph! The violins and harpsichord ring out an ornamented, celebratory hymn (rehearsal 12).

The rejoicing is short-lived; the texture evaporates, and the inane melody returns with the harpsichord clunking beneath (rehearsal 14). It feebly attempts a waltz, ignored by the violins, interrupted constantly by teeming strings (rehearsals 15–16). Time, melody, and motive are free.

During the steady buildup that follows, the basses and cellos adopt the waltz—fleshing it out with a sentimental melody—but are met with obsessive scrambling and obsessive repetition, not so much a tune as an obstinate stutter (rehearsal 17). Another ensemble episode—more menacing, staggered, and disjoined (rehearsal 19). The soloists strike the melody, chipping away at its gaps and crevices, before they and the ensemble fill them in with more echoes. But the repetitions overwhelm the clockwork (rehearsal 22). Stuck, wound too tightly, the machine spirals out of control and bursts (▶ audio 2.1).

*I*

In the Toccata, the past takes over. Schnittke bolstered the archaism of his composition's title—concerto grosso— by embracing another older form, one that, like the concerto grosso, flourished in the seventeenth and eighteenth centuries. Built on improvisation, on "touch" (the meaning of its Italian root), the toccata was almost exclusively a keyboard genre; it never featured as a movement in a concerto grosso.[1] A familiar example is J. S. Bach's Toccata and Fugue in D Minor for organ, a spooky Halloween standard that demonstrates many of the genre's characteristics: quasi-improvisational and virtuosic, it comprises several loose sections, brisk moments interspersed with gargantuan

ALFRED SCHNITTKE'S CONCERTO GROSSO NO. 1

Gothic chords (▶ audio 2.2). Rapid-fire twentieth-century precursors for Schnittke's interpretation of the genre include works or movements by Sergei Prokofiev, Claude Debussy, Maurice Ravel, Igor Stravinsky, and Aram Khachaturyan (▶ audio 2.3).

The concerto grosso—literally "big concerto"—itself attracted attention from several leading composers in the seventeenth and eighteenth centuries, among them Arcangelo Corelli, Antonio Vivaldi, and George Frideric Handel. It drew energy from a basic opposition between a group of soloists, the *concertino*, set off from the remainder of the ensemble, the *ripieno*, and contained multiple movements—from three to six—often including movements based on popular dance forms. Schnittke prized the genre because of its inherent drama, although he wavered on whether it emphasized cooperation or conflict.

Both concerto grosso and symphony fell by the wayside among leading composers striving for novelty in the first half of the twentieth century as they searched for new forms to reflect the all-too-new times. There are some exceptions, including compositions by Ernest Bloch and Ralph Vaughan Williams, for whom the concerto grosso represented a type of neoclassicism. And much like its avowed Bachian models—the Brandenburg Concertos—Stravinsky's Dumbarton Oaks Concerto in E-flat Major from 1937–38 could be considered a crypto-concerto grosso.

More symphonies than concerti grossi were written in the twentieth century, but the symphony became geographically constrained. At best, such leading modernists as Stravinsky, Anton Webern, and Arnold Schoenberg wrote veiled symphonies—symphonies that were not symphonies. Only, unexpectedly, did the symphony continue to thrive at the periphery of the dominating Germano-Romantic canon: in the Nordic countries (Jean Sibelius, Carl Nielsen), the United States (Aaron Copland, David Diamond, Samuel Barber, Roy Harris), and the Soviet Union (Prokofiev, Nikolai Myaskovsky, and Dmitri Shostakovich).

As a young, modernist-leaning composer struggling with the weighty, ideologically loaded tradition represented by the symphony in the Soviet Union, Schnittke remained ambivalent about writing an unmarked, unironic symphony. He often spoke of his initial, later-abandoned urge to name his Symphony no. 1 "a (non)-symphony," or, in German, "k(eine) Sinfonie." He set up dueling oppositions, calling it "symphony/anti-symphony" and "anti-symphony/symphony."[2] Even as he continued to write symphonies—he reached but did not surmount the fateful, Beethovenian number 9 just before his death—Schnittke kept calling into question the viability of a form so reliant on now-anachronistic tonal relations.[3] Yet for all his ironic equivocations about classical forms and classical tonality, Schnittke never flirted with labeling his Concerto Grosso no. 1 (or any of his subsequent essays in the genre) "k(ein) concerto grosso." The closest he came was his later Frankenstein-like grafting of the two genres—symphony and concerto grosso—in his Concerto Grosso no. 4/Symphony no. 5 (1988), a work not nearly as awkward as its title suggests, to which we will return in this book's final chapter.

Perhaps Schnittke was more confident in the concerto grosso than the symphony because of the numerous models he heard written by Eastern European composers from the 1950s onward. For these composers, it carried an air of foreignness—of being out-of-time—and carried fewer generic expectations. It lacked the pretensions to monumentality that clouded post-Beethovenian symphonism even as it maintained a classicized, less emotional respectability. At the 1956 Warsaw Autumn Festival, two compositions with "concerto grosso" in their titles were performed on the same day: Bolesław Szabelski's Concerto Grosso (1954) and Kazimierz Sikorski's Symphony no. 3 (1953), subtitled "In the Form of a Concerto Grosso."[4] In 1966, Schnittke's fellow Soviet composer Andrei Eshpai wrote his Concerto Grosso for trumpet, piano, vibraphone, bass, and orchestra—a jazzy blend of George Gershwin, Leonard Bernstein, Copland, and Stravinsky (⊙ audio 2.4). Lithuanian composer Julius Juzeliunas composed a concerto grosso published in 1968. But the nearest to Schnittke's Concerto Grosso no. 1, at least in terms of instrumentation, is the Concerto Grosso for Piano, Harpsichord, and Orchestra by Latvian composer Marģers (Marģeris) Zariņš from 1967. Not recorded until 1981 and published only in 1982 by the Leningrad section of the Sovetskii kompozitor publishing house, it includes a walking bass line and jazzy piano riffs at the end of its third movement and strong Stravinsky and Bartók influences overall. Noted late-Soviet composer Moisei (Mieczysław) Vainberg (Weinberg ) also wrote a concerto grosso, but he included it as the first movement ("Concerto Grosso") of his Symphony no. 10, op. 68, for chamber orchestra (1968). It is not clear that Schnittke knew any of these compositions. He never mentioned them, although at least the Eshpai and Weinberg works were probably on his radar.

These concerti grossi participated in the retrospective trend in Soviet and Eastern European music in the 1960s and 1970s, a trend parallel to simultaneous developments— a return to tonality, a return to the past—in Western Europe and America. Schnittke said that the movement titles of the Concerto Grosso no. 1 "carried a certain old-fashioned, stylized character."[5] Many composers in the Warsaw Pact countries also wrote music in self-consciously old or "retro" styles. Prominent examples include Polish composer Henryk Górecki's *Three Pieces in Old Style* (*Trzy utwory w dawnym stylu*, 1963), Polish composer Krzysztof Meyer's *Concerto Retro* (1976), and Schnittke's often-performed *Suite in the Old Style* for violin and piano (*Siuita v starinnom stile*, 1972), based on several of his film scores.[6]

Arvo Pärt was perhaps a stronger, closer influence on Schnittke's Concerto Grosso no. 1, with his series of compositions from the mid-1960s to the mid-1970s: *Collage on the Theme BACH* (1964), *Credo* (1968), and Symphony no. 3 (1971), among others. Schnittke said he heard the name "collage" attached to a piece of music for the first time with Pärt's composition, and both briefly pursued similar stylistic collisions in their music.[7] But despite lingering points of correspondence, by the time of their shared billing on a late-1977 tour of West Germany and Austria by the Lithuanian Chamber Ensemble, they had begun to seriously diverge stylistically.

## II

Schnittke wrote two accounts of the Concerto Grosso no. 1. We can call them his "Russian" and "German" program notes, based on the language in which they were first published. It is uncertain when precisely they were written; although neither was published before the mid-1980s or early 1990s, both appear to date from between 1977 and 1981.[8]

In 1977, Schnittke talked with East German musicologist Hannelore Gerlach about the Concerto Grosso no. 1, providing a datable point of comparison for both notes. At this time, Schnittke described the work as "multilayered" (*mehrschichtig*) and listed its musical components, emphasizing the contrasts to which it gave rise:

> One no longer finds serial techniques, but there are quasi-serial episodes and freely tonal themes. The texture is very tattered [*zerrissen*]: there are micropolyphonic sonic spaces [*Klangflächen*], a toccata reminiscent of both neoclassicism and Vivaldi and Corelli, a tango, and something like folk music— all of these are thematically linked with one another through certain intervals [*Intervallgruppen*]. Naturally the music is also stylistically multifaceted, but I believe that precisely from the confrontation and interplay of the different stylistic layers a certain tension develops that is then conveyed to the listener.[9]

In Schnittke's Russian program note for the Concerto Grosso no. 1, he spoke further about his motivations for writing the composition, motivations similar to those driving his development of polystylism. Rather than "confrontation" and "tension," he wrote of attempting to "bridge" the seemingly unbridgeable rifts within the contemporary soundscape, especially what he called the "gap between serious music and music for entertainment." He said, "It seems to me that there is a utopia consisting of a single style where fragments of serious music and fragments of music for entertainment would not just be scattered about in a frivolous way, but would be the elements of a diverse musical reality."[10]

He also noted the incongruous elements in the concerto grosso: "A lively children's chorale"; "a nostalgically atonal serenade—a trio guaranteed as genuine Corelli ('made in the USSR')"; and "my grandmother's favorite tango, which her great-grandmother used to play on a harpsichord."[11] The Russian program note was more flippant than his comments to Gerlach had been. But did the flippancy mask a sober message? He concluded with the assurance that "I take [all these themes] completely seriously."[12] Schnittke possessed a sly, often deadpan sense of humor, with all its associated pleasures and perils: his straight talk could be read as ironic, his ironic talk as straight.

His German program note covered some of the same territory but offered different characterizations of the instrumental forces in the Concerto Grosso no. 1. It also made decidedly negative claims about the role of popular music in its dramatic structure. Humor and sarcasm— and flippancy—seem to be absent. He called the prepared piano "an outside force" and spoke of "three musical spheres": "the codes and forms of Baroque music, freely tonal chromaticism and microintervals, and finally a banal type of vulgar Gebrauchsmusik."[13] "These three spheres are played against one another," he wrote. "The meaning of the 'Concerto' is also found here, and not only in the formal instrumental setting (soli versus tutti)."[14] He elaborated on his remarks about "music for use" (Gebrauchsmusik). "Banality has a fatal function in this piece," he said. "It actually cuts off all development and in the end it also triumphs. In our time, since the boldest and newest means already sound somehow dulled, in this kind of confrontation banality already achieves the expressiveness of a nearly demonic art."[15] But then Schnittke appeared to contradict himself:

> Yes, the banal belongs to life, and I find it not completely correct that for many years in the development of the avant-garde *trivialmusik* has been thrown out and ignored. Admittedly, in no case does the banal in my Concerto Grosso dominate with respect to time and space, but it, so to speak, works from without to disrupt and destroy.

His examples of banality in the work include the tango and the chorale theme, which he called the "sentimental song at the beginning that always recurs and, eventually, at the climax brings everything to ruin."

Schnittke further discussed the role of popular music—of "banality"—in the overall drama of the composition:

> The playing off of one another and interpolating of the different styles also provides significant stress in this piece. Yet there should not be a sharp, absolute demarcation of the spheres. But the "objective force of the banal" should be completely apparent, something like Thomas Mann describes in his "Tonio Kröger."[16]

Schnittke's dialectics are on full display in this note as he tacks between stress and strain, demarcation and interpolation, the demonic and the quotidian. Yet his appeal to Mann seems strange, for in "Tonio Kröger," Mann sets forth a more balanced presentation of banality's role in life and art, a sentiment more in line with the "utopian single style" from the Russian program note. But we will return to Mann's novella in due course.

Schnittke also wavered between conflict and cooperation. In a survey of his works published in 1990, musicologist Yevgeniya Chigaryova underscored the contrast inherent to the concerto grosso genre—and thus to Schnittke's composition. Yet Schnittke himself seems to have wanted the opposite. In a little-cited account of the piece from the late 1970s, a tape-recorded interview with his friend Arkady Petrov, Schnittke noted that he consciously chose the "old name concerto grosso," in which the soloists acted only as firsts among equals. They supported a "higher order," "a higher interrelationship between the orchestra and the soloists."[17] He distinguished this from the "type of interrelation between the soloists and orchestra" in the "classical or romantic concerto, where the relationship between the soloist and orchestra is built on contrasts and sometimes even on conflict, on drama." Instead, he said, "It is like in the old instrumental concertos of Bach, Vivaldi, and Corelli, where the soloist and orchestra—and even a group of soloists—play the exact same thematic material, not entering into a conflicting or contrasting relationship with the orchestra."[18] In this respect, the Concerto Grosso no. 1 counterbalanced the Symphony no. 1, in which, as he told Petrov, he had aimed to "collide" styles rather than "to synthesize" them.[19]

Schnittke's hesitations and qualifications across his various statements about the Concerto Grosso no. 1 highlight its dramatic tension between clarity and blending.[20] The score is immediately legible, its "separate spheres" obvious; a glance gives them away. This is a central characteristic of polystylism: its ready apprehension. Yet initial apprehensions deceive, blur, and bleed.

**III**

Schnittke's description of the First Concerto Grosso's constituent parts reveals only one layer of its musical construction. There is a rich, overdetermined corpus of sources informing its creation, among them Schnittke's fascinating sketches, which bring in a host of further themes and topics. These sketches raise more questions than they answer. We know very little about Schnittke's creative habits; few sketches survive for his works, except for those at Goldsmiths or in the Juilliard Manuscript Collection. Few detailed studies of those sketches have been published aside from Ivana Medić's instructive surveys of his Symphonies nos. 2 and 3.[21] Much more remains to be done.

It has been nearly a decade since first Jean-Benoît Tremblay and then Victoria Adamenko discussed Schnittke's sketches for the Concerto Grosso no. 1.[22] I have revisited these forty-one pages of sketches (in Russian with some German).[23] As Tremblay and Adamenko noted, they contain references by Schnittke to numerous banal binary pairings, including life and death, man and woman, "animus" and "anima," and, more surprisingly, Papageno and Papagena. Schnittke seems to have been intrigued by Carl Jung at the time: he labeled the orchestra the "collective unconscious" on one particularly dense, baffling sheet. There are other references to the "soul" and to the German Romantic tale *Peter Schlemiel* (1814) by Adelbert von

Chamisso, a "fairy tale" about a man who sells his shadow to a Mephistophilean figure.[24]

The sketch sheets are undated, but they appear to stem from early in the creative process, when Schnittke was first jotting down ideas. (Although early is a relative label given how quickly he reported writing it.) Nowhere in the sketches does he refer to the composition as a concerto grosso; two times he calls it "Concerto for 2 violins" (or "Concerto for 2 violins and orchestra"). The sketches include most of the main ideas of the piece: the main themes of the Toccata and the Rondo, the falling and rising minor-second motive from the Preludio (and elsewhere); the chorale theme; and the climactic reappearance of the chorale and the Butterfly cadence (e.g., movement 4, rehearsal 5, to be discussed further in chapter 4). Schnittke seems here to have been recording ideas as they came to him, freely associating as he first began to compose.

There are, as Tremblay notes, multiple versions of the movements and titles for the score (table 2.1). The sketches reveal Schnittke approaching its final arrangement. From the beginning, the Recitative and the Postlude were part of the scheme, but at one point, the Toccata was a Fugue and the movement following it was alternately Dialogue or Aria. The Rondo apparently was a late addition.

As intriguing are Schnittke's ideas about the "material" of the composition, its building blocks. One sheet (A4:10) lists four components in German:

1. Resolution—C with many overtones
2. Dissonances—atonality, glissandi, quarter-tones, aleatory, aperiodic rhythms

3. Quasi-diatonicism (beginning)—free groups of tones with second steps etc.
4. Dogmatic diatonicism

Another sheet (A4:3) lists four items in Russian. The first is challenging to decipher—perhaps "intonation in seconds" (*sekundovaia intonatsiia*)?—but numbers 2–4 match moments in the final score and show the central role that Schnittke gave popular music from the outset:

2. Chorale—to multiple-voiced cluster polyphony
3. Low genre—jazz violins, "Viennese Waltz," in the tavern/cabaret, etc. (with the harpsichord)
4. "Tonic" (only at the end!)
   (Schnittke listed a number 5, but left the space after it blank.)

Toward the bottom of this sheet (A4:3), he also noted that the chorale should have three "intonational variations": (1) diatonic, (2) chromatic, and (3) quarter-tone. From the beginning, Schnittke was interested in setting several layers of music in motion, and of those layers, the chorale, the waltz, and an unspecified "low genre" (in a tavern or cabaret) were to play central roles.[25]

Some of the musical themes in the sketches, most obviously the initials of Gidon Kremer and Tatiana Grindenko—the soloists and dedicatees—converted into musical notation, do not survive in the completed piece.[26] At no point in any of his later accounts of the composition, published or unpublished, does Schnittke refer to the other general concepts. And his notes about a

TABLE 2.1 Alfred Schnittke's discarded formal schemes for Concerto Grosso no. 1 (transcribed from sketches at Goldsmiths, University of London).

| A3:13 (bottom) | |
| --- | --- |
| I. Canon | I. Canon |
| II. Fuga | II. Fuga |
| III. Recitative (scratched out) | III. Recitative |
| IV. Dialogue (scratched out, Aria is written above) | IV. Aria |
| V. Drama | V. Chorale |
| VI. Postludia | VI. Development (*razrabotka*) |
| | VII. Postludia |
| A4:4 | |
| I. Introductory lyrical Prelude (*vstupitel'naia liricheskaia Preludiia*) (see Tremblay, "Polystylism," 147) | |
| II. [*liturgiia?*] (Toccata I) | |
| III. Chorale and recitative | |
| IV. Aria | |
| V. Toccata IV? Cadenza "Ural" [?] | |
| VI. Postludia | |
| A4:7 | |
| I. Praeludium | |
| II. Toccata | |
| III. Recitativo | |
| IV. Cadenza | |
| V. Finale | |
| VI. Postludium | |

"double-person"—the two soloists—pitted against the collective do not mesh with the statement he made to Petrov about the fundamental cooperation of the genre.

More pointedly, in a letter written the year after the Concerto Grosso no. 1 was finished and first performed, Schnittke rejected the very binary oppositions he had noted in the sketches. He wrote to Ukrainian composer Valentin Silvestrov (b. 1937) in January 1978:

> Recalling your list of pairs, I can say that for me there is no truth in a single one of the poles: neither drama nor prayer, neither picture nor icon, neither human nor godly, seems truthful when separated from its antithesis (just as, on another level, neither tonal nor atonal, neither thematic nor sonoristic, neither metrical nor syllabic, etc.). Can one of these poles become a way out? For me—no; for me each pole is a lie and a capitulation: either debauchery or castration.[27]

Needless to say, this emphatic pronouncement complicates some of the statements from the German program note, particularly his extreme remarks there about banality.

In his sketches, Schnittke made no indication of the extensive borrowed material in the score. When he jots down the Butterfly cadence and the chorale, he does not identify their sources. This is notable, for as Kholopova, among others, has observed, almost the entire Concerto Grosso no. 1 consists of already composed music.[28] Schnittke faced tight time constraints while writing the piece, and he apologetically admitted in his Russian program note that he had composed it unusually quickly: "Had anyone told me then that during the next year this would be performed several times and recorded, I would not have believed them, since for the most part I work very slowly, write many versions of a work, and never complete the first version."[29] One possibility is that in his rush, Schnittke turned to the pre-existing music to fill out the score. It represents an example of polystylism as expedient. Instead of rushing to fulfill a film commission with already composed "serious" music, Schnittke did the opposite.

As Schnittke told Petrov, the Concerto Grosso no. 1 draws from four film scores (three features and one cartoon) whose subjects include the legacy of Peter the Great; partisan warfare on the eastern front during World War II; Rasputin and the corrupt end of the Romanov dynasty; and environmentalism (the cartoon) (table 2.2). Although all had been written recently, these films form a motley assortment; they possess no common thread save their common creation by a talented composer working for hire. Schnittke said he chose these specific themes for the Concerto Grosso no. 1 because they share "a certain amount of intonational

TABLE 2.2 Film score sources for Alfred Schnittke's Concerto Grosso no. 1 (in chronological order).

| |
| --- |
| *Glass Harmonica (Stekliannaia garmonika)*, dir. Andrei Khrzhanovsky (1968) |
| *Butterfly (Babochka)*, dir. Andrei Khrzhanovsky (1972) |
| *Agony (Agoniia Rasputina)*, dir. Elem Klimov (1975/1984) |
| *The Tale of the Moor of Peter the Great* (*Skaz pro to, kak Tsar' Petr arapa zhenil*), dir. Alexander Mitta (1976) |
| *Ascent* (*Voskhozhdenie*), dir. Larisa Shepitko (completed 1976, released 1977) |

The dates for these films are taken from a variety of sources, including the films themselves; Richard Taylor, *The BFI Companion to Eastern European and Russian Cinema* (London: British Film Institute, 2009); Birgit Beumers, ed., *Directory of World Cinema: Russia* (Bristol: Intellect, 2011); and *Entsiklopediia kino* (2010), http://dic. academic.ru/contents.nsf/enc_cinema; and *Besedy,* 297–99 (2005).

commonality: they are related, they have one and the same melodic intervals, and therefore they fit together very logically."[30]

The 1972 cartoon *Butterfly* is a bald parable of the kind favored by its director, Andrei Khrzhanovsky. His *Glass Harmonica*, scored by Schnittke in 1968, argued on behalf of classical values—culture—against the corrupting influence of materialism.[31] *Butterfly* pits modernity—technology, the contemporary city, and the attempts by man to control the environment—against tranquility and a peaceful coexistence with nature. In it, a boy hunts and captures butterflies, only to be overwhelmed by them. Possessed by a nightmare vision of enveloping butterflies, he finally releases his samples. Beyond the spare yet memorable main theme—an exaggerated cadence—Schnittke might have considered using material from the cartoon because of its central neobaroque flute duet (⯈ video 2.1). Tremblay also points to *Glass Harmonica* as the source for the BACH references in the Concerto Grosso no. 1, noting that the appearance of the initials in the Rondo (rehearsal 10) uses the "same harmonization" as the cartoon.[32] But we cannot also discount as sources Schnittke's Piano Quintet (or Bach's own compositions and their many imitators).

*Agony* is a strange example of historical fiction. Like his mentor Mikhail Romm, its director, Elem Klimov, inserted documentary footage within his naturalistic depiction of the last days of the Romanovs, focusing on the debauchery of Rasputin. Rather than this particular tale, the memorableness of the tune—the tango—seems to have motivated Schnittke's appropriation of it from the film (⯈ video 2.2).

*The Tale of the Moor of Peter the Great* is a historical romp based on Alexander Pushkin's uncompleted novel *The Moor of Peter the Great* (*Arap Petra Velikogo*) about his own great-grandfather, Abram Gannibal, played with a wink by popular singer-actor Vladimir Vysotsky (in now-shocking blackface) and directed with a wink by Alexander Mitta. Mitta aimed to collide genres; he called the film an "alloy of tragedies and melodramas, adventure and psychological films."[33] In the Concerto Grosso no. 1, Schnittke drew the most from this film score. We have already noted its chorale, but Schnittke also mentioned "two active parts" that made their way into both the Toccata and the theme of the Rondo.[34] He meant the verse and chorus from the pop song at the outset of the film tracing Gannibal's journey from Africa to the retinue of Peter the Great. The song challenged Vysotsky, one of the most popular celebrities from the late Soviet period (rivaled perhaps only by Alla Pugachova). His musical renown stemmed from the gritty songs he growled over his own out-of-tune guitar playing. Schnittke asks him to stretch his voice, particularly in the leaping chorus, in which he only just reaches in a thin, forcibly sweet tone the very peaks of his range (▶ video 2.3).

The first excerpt from the Vysotsky song, the verse melody, appears in the initial episode of the Toccata after the palate-cleansing bass strikes (rehearsal 6), when the timbre, texture, and tone abruptly change (example 2.1; ▶ audio 2.5). The imitative violin soloists and harpsichord sound a fairy-tale elaboration of the verse's crucial half-step motto, inserting a slight flip before its descent. In the film, Vysotsky sings a variant of the violin's melody (without the flip) against a brief, bloody, colonialist cartoon

EXAMPLE 2.1    Alfred Schnittke, Concerto Grosso no. 1, movement 2, Toccata, rehearsal 6, first episode, quotation from *The Tale of the Moor of Peter the Great.*

explaining Gannibal's royal ancestry (he was son to an African king) and his capture by a rival tribe. The song has a rock swagger, prodded by a syncopated electric bass line and offbeat electric guitar chords. Its prominent harpsichord and solo violin interjections clearly foreshadow the Concerto Grosso no. 1 score. As Schnittke noted, he was impressively economical in his borrowing from this initial song; its saccharine chorus (now accelerated) became the first theme in the concerto grosso's Rondo, where we will next encounter it. (A transformed version of this chorus nearly identical to the Rondo theme appears in the film at the forty-minute mark.)

Schnittke said that he "used a great deal of music" from his score to Larisa Shepitko's film *Ascent*.[35] Yet this score consists of very little music. At most, in Concerto Grosso no. 1, there is a single brief borrowing from *Ascent* alongside some other general correspondences. The music from a crucial moment in the film appears in the Recitativo. At this point (1:21:00), the hero, Sotnikov, a former teacher turned artillery specialist, who is now imprisoned with other partisans (or those accused of being partisans), surveys them all, Christlike (▶ video 2.4). But the main theme in *Ascent*, with its repetitions, echoes, and webbed dissonances, also loosely resembles (in inversion) the descending, then rising violin theme from the Preludio and later the Recitativo.[36] At one point in his preparatory sketches, Schnittke jotted down material resembling this main theme from *Ascent* (A3:15). Yet the film score is much more bombastic and much less dissonant than anything in the Concerto Grosso no. 1. It also has broader resonances in Schnittke's output: the cues "Sotnikov's death" and (especially) "Remorse" resemble the Credo from Schnittke's Requiem, and the film's main theme also recalls the opening to his String Quartet no. 1, with its repetitions of a rising major second (C–D) (▶ audio 2.6–2.8).

What to do with all of this information? Tremblay, intrigued by what he called the "narrative potential" in the score, proposed a general narrative founded on the dualities (and other details) of the sketches.[37] Emphasizing the apocalyptic imagery in *Agony*, he relied heavily on the debatable idea that "Schnittke quotes himself because the excerpts he uses carry a similar meaning in different contexts."[38]

But the meanings of films do not usually transfer undiluted, if at all, to new works quoting from their music. No critics mentioned these earlier Schnittke films in their responses to Concerto Grosso no. 1. It would have been impossible for them to hear the traces of *Agony*, for no one had yet seen the film, which remained unreleased until the mid-1980s. The most prominent of the films in Schnittke's score was Mitta's (because of Vysotsky), so it is telling that Schnittke gave such pride of place in the Concerto Grosso no. 1 to the material from this film, as if begging for it to be recognized. The contexts of the chorale and the first song in *The Tale of the Moor of Peter the Great* prove false the idea that Schnittke used similar music in similar situations in both source and score. Despite the richness of its sonic narrativity, it seems a great stretch to interpret the Concerto Grosso no. 1 as both primal Russian homage and neocolonialist parable.

The Concerto Grosso no. 1 undoubtedly contains great narrative potential, but as we will see in the chapters to follow, the narratives Schnittke's early auditors accorded the composition are at odds with the specifics of Schnittke's sketches and with the films from which he drew most of his themes. They also diverge from Schnittke's other public and private statements about the work. More important than a specific narrative to the composition is the sense of "narrativeness" that it conveys. Schnittke spoke to Petrov about the broader influence of film on his creative approach to art music, particularly its effect on the "so-called drama of the musical composition." Rather than a "narrative type" of "dramaturgy," he said he relied on a dramaturgy that was "purely musical and founded on the relationships between themes, on their similarities and dissimilarities, on contrast, on the conflict of the themes, and on the tensions and climaxes that arise from the relationships between the themes." He also mentioned that the Symphony no. 1 "used a larger number of themes from my films."[39] Yet the quotations or stylizations in the Concerto Grosso no. 1 carry more weight thanks to their spare self-consciousness. Regardless of their sources, they sound like quotations, foreign in their immediate contexts.

## IV

The eruptive Toccata widens the emotional scope of the composition, rapidly accelerating from zero to sixty. As in historical toccatas such as Bach's, Schnittke's movement passes through a succession of sections. Its opening measures serve as a frame of reference to which the music returns in whole or in part throughout its course. Kholopova noted the influence of Vivaldi at the start, but the influences are much broader—in Schnittke's Toccata, baroque counterpoint runs amok.[40] Or, rather, baroque counterpoint is inflected using twentieth-century techniques, particularly those of Ligeti, Schoenberg, and Webern. Micropolyphony, or intricate webs of temporally close canons (as in mm. 6–13) and twelve-tone structures are interspersed with pastiche eighteenth-century music.

In measure 78 (rehearsal 14), the BACH motive makes its first prominent appearance in the Concerto Grosso no. 1 (the first of many), this time as the opening pitches in a twelve-tone row, a self-consciously naïve setting accompanied by a waltzlike harpsichord pattern (example 2.2). Rather than strictly according to the book, this section is "twelve-tonish": the second violin traces a descending chromatic scale with an octave displacement in measure 79; and the harpsichord begins with a transposed, intervallically collapsed yet exploded variant of the B♭–A–C–B♮ motive, now E♭–D♭–E♮–D♮, with the two middle pitches sounded simultaneously. (If completely transposed, it would be: E♭–D–F–E♮.) It continues with a registrally scattered descending chromatic scale, the first four pitches of which are a reshuffling of the BACH motive (C–B♮– B♭–A).[41]

The waltzing, twelve-tone BACH reference occurs just after the high point of the Toccata and of the Concerto Grosso no. 1 up to this moment: at rehearsal 12, the clouds clear, and the sun briefly emerges. We hear a reprise of the opening chorale in the harpsichord, under passagework in the solo violins, with solo violin 1 also tracing the chorale's top pitches an octave higher (⊙ audio 2.9). It is a challenging moment to perform; not all recordings make this return clear. It is nearly inaudible on both the Kremer

EXAMPLE 2.2  Alfred Schnittke, Concerto Grosso no. 1, movement 2, Toccata, rehearsal 14, twelve-tone, BACH waltz, measures 78–80.

and Grindenko Deutsche Grammophon recording and the Krysa and Isakadze Melodiya recording but clearer on the Kuleshov and Ioff Bomba St. Petersburg disc (see appendix).

The chorale's reappearance does not last long, culminating quickly in a dissonant pileup and aleatory slides in measure 77, before veering in measure 78 back to Bach, Schoenberg, and the waltz. The swiftly alternating moments of cooperation and conflict in the Concerto Grosso no. 1 explain why Schnittke's own thinking about the composition kept changing. As much as anyone, he could be stirred by the freewheeling fantasies evoked by his "purely musical dramaturgy."

Musicologist Peter Burkholder memorably described the final section of the Toccata, in which "the stylistic contrasts in the movement are resolved paradoxically, with all the themes coexisting, but in a modernist world of maximum density and complexity."[42] Maximum tension leads to breakdown. Whether modernist or postmodernist, at this stage of his career, Schnittke the polystylist loved such dramatic juxtapositions—pushing things to their limits, whether rhythmically, formally, or harmonically through piled-up themes and dissonances—as is evident in the Concerto Grosso no. 1 on all levels. Schnittke also highlighted the opposition between stillness and activity, demonstrated already by the concerto grosso's first two movements. This oscillation continues throughout the concerto grosso, propelling it to its uncertain end. The activity proved as unsettling as the stillness, although together both ultimately held out hope of redemption.

# CHAPTER 3

## *RECITATIVO*

A NOTHER EMOTIONAL WHIPLASH: FROM the Toccata's propulsion, a darker turn. First, only the ensemble: somber waves, impulses, urges. Slide and smear, an inversion of the violins' first entrances in the Preludio, ascent preceding descent. The soloists—subdued—echo but grow frustrated (rehearsal 1, example 3.1). Foreground and background struggle to separate, grasp for distinctions. The solo violins interject aching dissonances, continued fragments of earlier sounds (rehearsal 3). Gesture dominates form. The back and forth between soloists and ensemble becomes more consequential.

Again, stillness. Agonized breathing. Obscure motion below, a kind of ground bass, but soloists and ensemble remain cut off (rehearsal 5). Steadily mounting, tense—more frenzied (rehearsals 7–10). Glissandi across the grouping

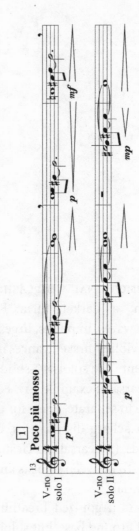

EXAMPLE 3.1    Alfred Schnittke, Concerto Grosso no. 1, movement 3, Recitativo, violin soloists, rehearsal 1, measures 13–17.

reach a sudden climax: Tchaikovsky's Violin Concerto emerges from the mists, soon swamped by swirling incomprehension (rehearsal 11). Resolution? None (⊙ audio 3.1).

*

What does the title of this movement mean? A recitative in eighteenth- and nineteenth-century opera advanced the plot. Usually, text sung in recitative was set more or less syllabically and therefore moved more briskly than the words luxuriated over in arias—the real crowd-pleasing moments of operatic songfulness. But Schnittke's recitative does not convey anything beyond a worrying over familiar fragments. It is a collision, a vocal genre in an instrumental composition, and an anachronism: despite the many borrowings between instrumental and vocal music in the seventeenth and eighteenth centuries, none of the movements in Vivaldi's, Corelli's, or Handel's concerti grossi was called "recitative."[1]

Many critics heard an exaggerated vocality in this movement, the most tormented in the Concerto Grosso no. 1. Kholopova called it "serious, filled with the intonations of lamenting, of grief," and Don Anderson described it as "a dark funereal lament."[2] Other critics noticed only darkness: Harvey Sachs said it was "a nightmarishly bleak landscape," and Richard Tiedman referred to "the cavernous glooms and heavily endemic grief of the Recitative."[3] Oleh Krysa considers the third and fourth movements the core of the work.[4] The Recitativo vies with the Rondo as the longest movement in the composition (both clock in at around seven minutes). It is the grim center from whose gravity the rest of the work struggles to break free.

While the anxiety mounts over the course of the movement, ultimately, the solo violinists break down and scramble for a stable foothold. Rehearsals 6–8 are a study in sonority: strings circle dissonantly around a restricted space, pushing quarter-tones beyond familiar pitches, creating friction (▶ audio 3.2). At rehearsal 9, sparks shower forth from the solo violins. In the section from rehearsals 10–11, both instruments are given only approximate renderings of what they are meant to perform. Typically, one voice plays a precisely notated figuration while the other quasi-improvises against it. The swoops in the second violin from measures 96–97 are particularly suggestive—stereotypical ghosts (▶ audio 3.3). The violins latch finally onto the second theme from movement 1 of Tchaikovsky's Violin Concerto (rehearsal 11, m. 102), with a hurried glimpse of Berg's Violin Concerto shortly thereafter (m. 106, example 3.2; ▶ audio 3.4–3.6).[5] But this is too little too late. The tension continues to build as the two violins slowly converge: at maximum volume, violin 1 trills downward, and violin 2 slides chromatically upward. At measure 110, having crossed, they both blurt out a final exclamation. Then the page turns, and the next movement begins.

One of the largest questions posed by this movement concerns the Tchaikovsky and Berg quotations. Why are they there? Chigaryova calls the Tchaikovsky quotation "false," an "unrecognizably distorted theme" that "sounds like a symbol of a support that might have been [neosushchestvivshaiasia opora]."[6] Perhaps both references arose by chance: Schnittke noticed the similarities to his

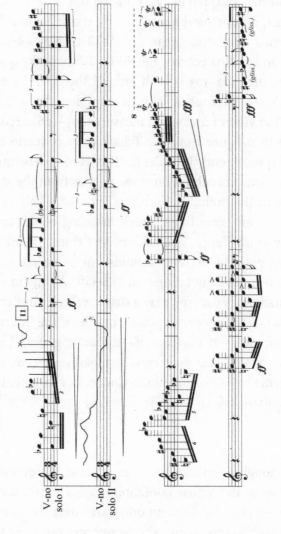

EXAMPLE 3.2    Alfred Schnittke, Concerto Grosso no. 1, movement 3, Recitativo, Tchaikovsky and Berg quotations, measures 101–107.

own music at that moment and added them. He likely planned a climax at this point involving some kind of tonal material, and Tchaikovsky fit the bill. But the fit was not exact; he doctored his source by transposition. The result carried symbolic meaning. As Tremblay observed, the second violin's echo of the initial Tchaikovsky quotation in measures 102–103 is built around the BACH motive (two measures after rehearsal 11 in example 3.2).[7]

The violin 1 melody in measures 105–106, a reworking of the turn figure from the Tchaikovsky concerto quotation, also prominently includes the BACH motive before moving, via a transition built on three pitches from the stalled motive in the Preludio (with the E♭ raised a half-step: C♯–E♮–D), to an exceedingly quick intoning of the twelve-tone row from Berg's Violin Concerto (mm. 15–18). Whether long planned or serendipitous—or some combination of the two—the quotations, and specifically the more audible Tchaikovsky excerpt, play a structural role similar to the reprise of the prepared piano chorale in the Toccata. It is a brief, clear—if misleading—climactic gesture.[8] (Schnittke had quoted the Berg row in measures 64–65 of his cadenza to Beethoven's Violin Concerto, movement 1, but not Tchaikovsky's concerto.)

## II

Although Schnittke has a reputation for quotations and collages, the actual quotations in his music are comparatively rare and became only rarer over the course of the late 1970s and 1980s. The Symphony no. 1 contained the greatest number of actual quotations, near-quotations, and pastiches in his output, with his *Serenade* and Violin Sonata no. 2, "Quasi una Sonata," following close behind. After this grouping of late-1960s and early-1970s compositions, Schnittke reserved his most blatant references for significant moments—as he does in nearly every movement of the Concerto Grosso no. 1. Schnittke seemed to realize that despite his emphasis on "poly"—on multiplicity—less was often more.

The retreat from quotations in Schnittke's music did not result in a diminishing of its narrative force. Quite the contrary: he still used stylistic clashes to convey, well, something. Yet his signifying gestures moved closer to the type of messaging more familiar from Dmitri Shostakovich's later music, in which isolated quotations subsisted in murky, emotionally fraught settings, as with the excerpts from Gioachino Rossini's *William Tell* and Richard Wagner's *Götterdämmerung* in his Symphony no. 15 (1971) (⊙ audio 3.7).

Although Schnittke spoke openly in the mid-1980s of the "shadow sounds" (*Schattenklänge*) in his music, his style was already growing more shadowy in the mid-1970s. There had been premonitions in his earlier music, too: he spoke of the "Canon" movement of his String Quartet no. 1 as "having a diffluent character, decreasing with false shadows and reflections (false because in the reflections they already contain other notes)."[9]

In the early 1970s, Schnittke prominently evoked shadows in his essay on György Ligeti's use of micropolyphony, a device we first encountered in the Toccata and that also pervades the Recitativo and many other moments in the Concerto Grosso no. 1. For Schnittke, micropolyphony was a flexible approach; it was often highly dissonant but was not necessarily so. It could be fast or slow—a soft, slippery cascade or a whirling swarm—both extremes conveying, as Schnittke seems to have preferred, gradations of unease, multiple, quick iterations of an idea, like a glitch in the matrix.

In his study of Ligeti's use of this device in *Lontano*, Schnittke observed: "The listener is enveloped in the most delicate web of sound through which, like distant phantoms, appear familiar shadows of romantic music."[10] Schnittke was consistently drawn to phantoms, shadows, and glimmers of the past in the present. Micropolyphony evoked all three.

He was drawn not just to darkness. Schnittke also prized interactions between light and dark:

> Sometimes they [the familiar shadows of romantic music] become clearer and come into focus in dazzling beams of light, heralding a miracle, but at the last moment the golden nimbus fades and everything mists over. Now the mist thickens, then we see sharply defined dark shapes, but the gloom proves as unstable as the light. Everything is unsteady, full of meaning, elusive.[11]

The light held specific metaphysical meaning for Schnittke: "As in Plato's cave we glimpse only reflections of a higher reality, but we are powerless to grasp it. As in a dream, we hear only echoes of some vast sonorous world, but on awakening, we cannot remember it." As he said, Ligeti realized in *Lontano* "a mirage in sound."[12] Micropolyphony encapsulated Schnittke's emerging Neoplatonic sense of creativity and existence. The Concerto Grosso no. 1 further explored its sonic implications. The

Ligeti essay also revealed the other side of Schnittke's attraction to micropolyphony: it required "precise calculation." As his sketches reveal, Schnittke continued prizing both intuition and contrivance.[13]

## III

Schnittke's early attraction to shadows becomes clearest in his reference to a novella about shadows in the sketches for the Concerto Grosso no. 1. Perhaps it is not worth paying much attention to an isolated scribble. Yet the story of "Peter Schlemiel" resonates with the sounding surface of the Concerto Grosso no. 1 and reinforces Schnittke's other statements from the time about shadows and spirits.

Schlemiel, meant by the novella's writer, Aldebert von Chamisso, to evoke the Jewish archetype of the "clumsy or unlucky souls who succeed at nothing in this world," sells his shadow to a mysterious man in gray, a self-described "poor devil, a sort of sage and alchemist."[14] The result forces Schlemiel to waver between laughter and terror, as when a young women he desires discovers his secret: "Aghast, she looked up at me in horror, then down at the ground again, searching for my absent shadow; and her train of thought was so legible in her troubled look that I would have burst out in loud laughter had a cold chill not then and there run down my spine."[15] Such traumatic encounters lead Schlemiel to realize the error of his ways. He tries to reclaim his shadow, at which point the man in gray agrees to return it—but only in exchange for Schlemiel's soul. The connection between shadow and soul is made explicit: "I've got you by your shadow . . . no

sense trying to escape. A rich man like you needs a respectable shadow, there's no getting around it." Or as a
young boy says, sneering, earlier in the novella: "Honest
people don a shadow when they step out into the sun"
(figures 3.1–3.2).[16]

Refusing to make the exchange, Schlemiel finds redemption in nature and science. Through a plot contrivance, he

FIGURES 3.1 AND 3.2   Images by George Cruikshank from Chamisso's "Peter
Schlemihl" (London: G. and W. B. Whittaker, 1824).

FIGURES 3.1 AND 3.2 Continued.

acquires a pair of magical—seven-league—boots that allow
him to travel speedily to the ends of the earth. Ultimately,
he "gain[s] a deeper knowledge and learn[s] more than any
man before me of the earth, its formation, its precipices, its
atmospheres in their constant flux, the manifestations of its
magnetic force and its life forms, particularly the flora." The

moral is clear: "But to you, my dear friend, I say that if you wish to live among your fellow man, learn to value your shadow more than gold."[17]

Perhaps Schnittke did not pursue the idea of Schlemiel beyond its most cursory outlines because of the basic difference between novella and composition: Schlemiel is about a man who loses his shadow, and the Concerto Grosso no. 1 is about shadows tightly bound one to the next. The clearest resonance between novella and composition comes during Schlemiel's bargaining for his soul's return, when the mysterious man in gray torments Schlemiel with his shadow:

> He proceeded to pull my shadow out of his pocket and, with a skilful toss, unfurled it on the heath and spread it out on the sunny side at his feet so that he could stride up and down in between the two shadows, his and mine; mine had to obey, to twist and turn in accordance with his every move.[18]

Here the shadow represents a crossing over from good to evil, a selfishness that leads to a loss of self. But aside from any moral connotations, the dance Chamisso describes from one shadow to the next, twisting and turning, can be heard without much difficulty in many of the concerto grosso's darker moments, chief among them the Recitativo. This is the most shadowy of the six movements, with multiple layers of reflections, refractions, and shading between the two soloists and between the soloists and the ensemble.

Schnittke's flirtation with Schlemiel says more in a general sense about his taste than about any specific programmatic connection between concerto grosso and novella. Interpreting the two solo violins as figure and shadow or the pervasive micropolyphony in the Concerto Grosso no. 1 as a prismatic refraction of sounds—a chord containing everything split into its constituent, shadowing elements—is too easy. More compelling are the novella's romantic themes. Schlemiel as a Faust figure found embodiment in several of Schnittke's most important works from the ensuing decades: his *Faust Cantata* (*Seid nüchtern und wachet . . .*, 1983), his Faust opera (*Historia von D. Johann Fausten*, 1983–94), and his *Peer Gynt* ballet (1986). Schnittke's sensibility skewed dark. He was drawn increasingly to shadows and echoes, reflections and mirrors, the idea of the soul divided against itself, cast out but, at the last moment, redeemed.

As his German program note indicates, Schnittke started with Schlemiel but landed on Thomas Mann's "Tonio Kröger," which he did not mention in his surviving sketches. Mann's novella more directly engaged with themes central to this composition and to Schnittke's output from the 1970s and 1980s, particularly issues of personal (national and ethnic) identity but also the status of popular styles and genres in his music. From this point, rather than embracing high and low as interwoven, equally necessary, if utopian, parts of the contemporary soundscape, Schnittke spoke more often of banality, especially in the Concerto Grosso no. 1. While the Recitativo's Tchaikovsky quotation, and much of the Toccata, might be heard as an elevation of the banal, that description applies most blatantly to the Rondo. We will return more directly to it in that context.

## CHAPTER 4

# CADENZA

S EAMLESSLY, THE SOLO VIOLINS replay the descending and rising discordances from the Preludio. Deprived of an aria, we get a cadenza. If a recitative carries certain expectations of voice, plot, and communication, cadenzas are equally freighted with meanings: virtuosity, excess, transport. Schnittke's Cadenza asks more questions than it answers, foreshadowing introspection rather than extroversive display—or, rather, an extroversive display of introversion.

Difficult to describe, in the Cadenza, disharmony and unity clash. Melody is scarcely discernible. More arresting is the turn to pizzicato at rehearsal 2; it is the first time the soloists play using this technique, dissecting and atomizing the falling and rising gesture from the Preludio. Chigaryova justifiably calls it a "hypertrophied" pizzicato.[1] But we soon return to straining and wailing. Chigaryova also mentions the "severe, whining/howling/screeching intonations of the violins"—all are possible translations of the Russian *podvyvaiushchie*—and all seem appropriate for this movement.[2] Sharp attacks spin into trills, then delicate melody, a glimpse of grace. At times, the two soloists seem like a single hypertrophied instrument; at other times, as in the second violin's entrance after measure 24, they attack or undercut each other. Breakdown again leads to calamity—but then a sudden CADENCE!—a forced resolution of something irresolvable (⊕ audio 4.1).

## *I*

Primed by Schnittke's sketch, we hear shadows everywhere. This briefest of movements is a shadow of a cadenza. Such moments were not a standard part of concertos, grosso or otherwise, in the late seventeenth and early eighteenth centuries. The famous harpsichord cadenza in movement 1 of Bach's Brandenburg Concerto no. 5 is the exception that proves the rule. Cadenzas, like recitatives, were more often found in vocal music. Thus, there is loose, vocal-based continuity between movements 3 and 4 of Schnittke's concerto. More likely, Schnittke, influenced by the nineteenth-century virtuoso concerto repertoire, wanted to foreground his star soloists. But there also were precursors among his own compositions: he called the final movement of his String Quartet no. 1 "Cadenza." Another possible explanation hinges on the ending of this particular Cadenza. Cadenzas have their roots in embellished cadences, and this particular Cadenza ends with a big one. Perhaps Schnittke wanted to accord his Butterfly cadence (rehearsal 5) added structural and emotional heft by preceding it with a reinterpreted expansion of what "classically" would have preceded it (example 4.1; ⊙ audio 4.2).

The focus on the soloists at this moment offers an opportunity to consider the performers and the initial performances of Schnittke's Concerto Grosso no. 1. Saulius Sondeckis (1928–2016), the Lithuanian conductor, said that the work was a loose "commission" from Gidon Kremer. Schnittke's compensation was not monetary but symbolic: Kremer's goal was to force a new Soviet composition, and particularly one by Schnittke, on official orchestral tours outside the Soviet Union.[3] Up to that point, Schnittke had rarely been heard beyond its borders.

For that matter, he was rarely heard within those borders, although heard he was. Kremer was a prime stimulus for what performances he did receive, for the violinist scheduled Schnittke performances when he could, particularly of his Violin Sonata no. 2. As Schnittke later wrote in admiration (and perhaps envy), "Gidon Kremer always gets what he wants."[4] After all, Kremer, who had studied with David Oistrakh at the Moscow Conservatory, had won the 1970 Tchaikovsky Competition and received a laudatory reception in Europe, particularly from Herbert von Karajan, who pronounced him "the greatest violinist in the world."[5]

Kremer played a key role not only in the concerto grosso's inception but also its dissemination and eventual renown. In a 1976 interview, as he prepared to write the Concerto Grosso no. 1, Schnittke acknowledged Kremer as "an unbelievable boom [sic] for me, because he has

EXAMPLE 4.1   Alfred Schnittke, Concerto Grosso no. 1, movement 4, Cadenza, Butterfly cadence, rehearsal 5, measures 25–end.

performed my compositions probably hundreds of times (everything but the first [violin] concerto)."[6] He compared Kremer to violinist Mark Lubotsky, for whom he had composed almost all his previous violin works, including both Violin Concerto no. 1 and no. 2 and Violin Sonata no. 1 and no. 2: "for Kremer . . . it will be a completely different kind of music than what I wrote for Lubotsky because I cannot but take into account the character of the performer: Kremer is much stronger in terms of instrumental technique; and in terms of performative and intonational tension he is also more profound than Lubotsky."[7]

Sofia Gubaidulina, who wrote another of Kremer's calling cards, her concerto *Offertorium* (1983), also praised his sensitivity: he "has such a great inner plasticity and very intimate touch to the string. And it's that intimate touch that left me speechless. His ability to touch the string as if he is giving birth to a new being because of the way he is caressing the strings."[8] Svetlana Savenko called him a "violinist with a universal stylistic range."[9] A German critic enthused: "Kremer embodies in a lightly articulated, delicate way an infinitely sensitive, depressive, yet very late-Romantic type of virtuoso." Furthermore, he wrote, "Kremer's extraordinariness is that he indeed rules and commands all these romantic voices, feelings, and resources." The same reviewer also noted parenthetically that Tatiana Grindenko was "a good violinist, not very inferior to Kremer."[10]

Grindenko was certainly no slouch. She played a startling range of musical styles and genres, from popular and avant-garde to the standard classical repertoire (what Russians often refer to as "academic music"). Grindenko took part in performances by the rock group Boomerang (Bumerang) at the Scriabin Museum electronic music studio in Moscow in the early 1970s, and as she later recounted, she "participated in one of the first performances of Valentin Silvestrov's *Drama* and played music by John Cage and Karlheinz Stockhausen."[11] She said: "My violin could sound in various ways, among them also like a normal violin. Thus for me Alfred Schnittke's Concerto Grosso [no. 1] was like a piece of absolutely academic music and therefore I didn't completely understand the tizzy it caused among academic musicians." She later elaborated: "We carted [the Concerto Grosso no. 1] around the entire world, but from the very first that work did not come as a shock to me. What shocked me was another composition of Alfred's that I also played, 'Quasi una sonata,' but now that is practically academic music."[12]

Schnittke himself commented about his two dedicatees, Kremer and Grindenko: "Wonderful musicians; although completely distinct in their creative individuality, they often perform as a well-honed duet in which both their individual capabilities and their cohesion mutually reinforce one another." He continued, describing exactly what individual capabilities he had in mind: Kremer was a "large-scale concertizing violinist, but also strict and reserved," and Grindenko was "sharp and nervous with tension in the details." "And in writing the concerto," Schnittke said, "not only did I hear them, but I also saw how they play—after all, the behavior of musicians on the stage is also significant. In this case, their behavior was aesthetically pleasurable for both listeners and viewers" (figure 4.1).[13]

FIGURE 4.1   Tatiana Grindenko and Gidon Kremer, Bach Double Concerto LP cover (Eurodisc/Melodia SQ 28 515 KK, 1977).

Savenko amplified these comments in her liner notes to the Melodiya release of Kremer and Grindenko's first recording of Concerto Grosso no. 1: "The soloists' parts are absolutely equal and often give the impression that a single violin with many strings is playing." Suggesting that she knew of Schnittke's musings about shadows, she remarked, "ideal intonation and equality of bowing in the performance subtly appear in the numerous canonic episodes in which the second voice appears like a sonic shadow, the double of the first, creating the effect of its own kind of spatiality, an echo." Savenko provides another interpretation of the shadows in the work: they are a result of near-perfect playing. Not just figure and shadow, the violins are uncanny doubles, an image that recalls a host of Russian literary forebears—Fyodor Dostoevsky's *The Double*, a tale of a haunting doppelgänger, first and foremost, followed closely by its progenitor, Nikolai Gogol's "The Nose." Complicating the messaging was the personal intertwining of the two soloists: Kremer and Grindenko had once been married.

## II

Schnittke began composing his Concerto Grosso no. 1 in May 1976 and completed the first version on January 21, 1977. He revised it later that spring.[14] He said in the Russian program note that he gave the first version to Kremer for his thirtieth birthday on February 27, 1977.[15] This version premiered in Leningrad on March 21, 1977, in the Small Hall of the Leningrad Philharmonic, with Eri Klas conducting the Leningrad Chamber Orchestra and Kremer, Grindenko, and Yuri Smirnov as soloists.[16] Sondeckis reports that some "deficiencies" in both the score and its interpretation became apparent at this performance, but "no doubts arose": with the necessary revisions, "the work could be hugely successful."[17]

The second version, the result of "several cuts," premiered shortly thereafter on April 12, 1977, in Vilnius, Lithuania, with the same soloists but now with Sondeckis conducting the Lithuanian Chamber Orchestra.[18] In the Russian program note, Schnittke reported that Kremer and Grindenko then performed it in Vilnius, Moscow, Riga, Tallinn, and Budapest, as well as in August at the Salzburg Festival with the London Symphony Orchestra and Gennady Rozhdestvensky.

In a later reminiscence, Sondeckis discussed in greater detail the Moscow performances that Schnittke mentioned. Sondeckis had planned for the work to be included on the Lithuanian Chamber Orchestra's subscription series in Moscow at the Large Hall of the Moscow Conservatory in April 1977. But he initially met with resistance. Schnittke's music was struck from the program for what the authorities alleged were procedural reasons: it had yet to be properly vetted by the Union of Composers. (Schnittke constantly encountered this type of obstruction and obfuscation well into the 1980s.)[19] Yet, Sondeckis reports, the artistic director of the Moscow Philharmonic (the concert organization, not the orchestra), pianist A. Kuznetsov, intervened and allowed Schnittke's Concerto Grosso no. 1 to be included. The nature of the composition, and its innocuous title, likely helped. The taming of his First Symphony's free-for-all effects, the concerto grosso's reduced instrumental forces, and its propulsive, familiar Toccata all likely weighed in its favor.

The rehearsals took place in Vilnius, where, Sondeckis reported, he, Schnittke, Kremer, Grindenko, and the orchestral musicians "worked tensely, with everyone placing great demands upon themselves." Sondeckis had only positive comments about Schnittke's role: he rarely interfered in the rehearsal process, pausing only here and there to comment on the "colors of the sounds, the character of the bowing, and tempo modifications." Overall, Sondeckis said, "He gave more freedom to his performers than many other composers."[20]

Before the official performance at the Moscow Conservatory, the ensemble had been enlisted to play at the

Physics Institute of the Academy of Sciences (Fizicheskii Institut Akademii Nauk, or FIAN), a central, albeit restricted, venue for new music since the 1960s. (FIAN was not open to the general public, and one needed connections to attend performances there.) Sondeckis remembered this test run of the Concerto Grosso no. 1 because the "disgraced" scientist Andrei Sakharov, shunned for his outspokenness on human rights but nonetheless still a member of the institute, listened on a couch in the corner.

Sondeckis keenly recalled the next day's public performance:

> It's difficult to describe the atmosphere at Schnittke's concert in the Large Hall of the Moscow Conservatory! It was a sensation! All of musical Moscow flocked to the Large Hall. As the saying goes, people were hanging from the rafters. The lucky ones who had tickets packed into the hall until they were turned away. People stood in all the entryways, anywhere they could squeeze in. Only Stravinsky's appearance [in 1962] or the first tours of American orchestras [to the Soviet Union in the late 1950s] had aroused such interest.[21]

Seemingly hyperbolic, Sondeckis conveys the energy that surrounded Schnittke's music at the time. The question was whether this energy would translate into a positive decision from the Soviet artistic bureaucracy about including the work on the ensemble's tour to Europe later in the year. But the answers were affirmative; the Ministry of Culture even agreed to pay for the work, apparently a first for Schnittke at the time. Their response was typical and worth noting: "Who is spreading the rumor that we are against Schnittke? We're only against bad music. . . . But if someone writes a good composition we will recommend that it be purchased and support its application to Goskontsert for performance abroad."²² Such bureaucratic disingenuousness was commonplace in the late Soviet Union.

Grindenko noted with surprise that

> not only circles of musicians were thrown into a tizzy [by Schnittke's composition], but also, so to speak, official circles, because they didn't know whether to approve it or not. But, thank God, the fate of the Concerto Grosso no. 1 was very fortunate. From the very first moment that composition was practically given the green light and it turned out, in general, to be very successful and pleased everyone: the public, the powers that be, the left, the right—everyone, from all walks of life, such a complete success [*stoprotsentnoe popadenie v desiatku*].

Grindenko added, "I also liked that music very much; it was a pleasure to play."²³

This was a common response. Oleh Krysa said something similar: "Everything was done so masterfully by Schnittke; it was a masterful composition." He said that the Concerto Grosso no. 1 never required much rehearsal; it was very easy to perform because everything fit together so well. Schnittke was not a violinist but wrote very much like one, Krysa observed. "It was a pleasure to perform and always had unbelievable success with audiences."²⁴

## III

Kremer later said the decision to take the Concerto Grosso no. 1 abroad was both his and Schnittke's:

Not only did we give the first performance together, but we also had the idea of going abroad together. And at that time, since I enjoyed relative independence in intolerable circumstances, I managed somehow to put the idea into practice and to involve a pianist no one had heard of, Alfred Schnittke, so that he could see the world. I thought that this was not just wonderful for us (the composer was actually performing) but simply essential as far as he was concerned.[25]

Kremer's account makes the arrangement out to be simpler than it was. Sondeckis recalled tense, convoluted, bureaucratic negotiations over Schnittke's participation in the tour. No sooner had Sondeckis succeeded in having the inclusion of Schnittke's composition in the planned programs approved by Goskontsert than he realized Kremer wanted Schnittke to accompany them on the tour not as a composer but as the keyboard player with the orchestra, performing both piano and harpsichord parts in his own score and the piano part in Arvo Pärt's *Tabula Rasa*. Sondeckis said, "Upon receiving our request, and not anticipating such impertinence, the Soviet Union of Composers literally roared: 'What gall! It's not enough that we decided to allow this piece to be taken abroad, he himself wants to go to the capitalist lands [*kapstrana*]? Who among our composers, even the leading ones, accompanies the performers of his works abroad? And here Schnittke wants to."[26]

They asked, "Is it really true that there isn't another pianist who can play the piano and harpsichord parts?" Stuck, Sondeckis lied through his teeth: he claimed that the piano parts were not written down and that only Schnittke knew them, a fable that easily could have been disproved, because at the April 14 performance of the Concerto Grosso no. 1 in

Moscow, another pianist had played the part from a fully notated score. But the bureaucrats failed to perform due diligence and never discovered this.[27]

More powerful as an argument was the anticipation for Schnittke's score already building abroad, bolstered by Kremer's strong reputation in Europe and the reputation of Sondeckis as well. For the orchestra Sondeckis directed from the National M. K. Čiurlionis School of Art in Vilnius had won first prize in 1976 at the Herbert von Karajan Foundation Youth Orchestra competition held in West Berlin. Kremer also suggested that the plan succeeded because some of the necessary bureaucratic documents were completed and submitted in Lithuania, one of the more liberal Soviet republics. Sondeckis added that it would have been too difficult to replace Schnittke's composition with another Soviet work so late in the process, as 50 percent of the music for Soviet tours abroad had to consist of Soviet music.[28]

Further meetings ensued in Moscow with Kremer and Schnittke. But Schnittke himself, Sondeckis recalled, cared less about his own participation, declaring, "Most important for me is the performance of my composition." To the surprise of all, both the Concerto Grosso no. 1 and Schnittke were allowed to remain on the tour; there were no last-minute "illnesses" among the musicians (a standard practice for preventing undesirable figures from leaving the Soviet Union). They flew to Europe on November 13, 1977.[29]

Kremer said that before the trip, "Schnittke was completely overwhelmed and very nervous, because he had never performed in public."[30] For Schnittke, the trip was "very interesting, but very tiring: 28 days with daily rehearsals and 22 concerts."[31] Sources disagree over exactly how many concerts there were on this tour and how many times Concerto Grosso no. 1 was performed. Sondeckis wrote that it was played in twenty of the orchestra's twenty-four concerts in West Germany and in Austria, including Mannheim, Frankfurt am Main, Karlsruhe, Regensburg, Munich, Augsburg, Stuttgart, Hanover, Bonn, Essen, Wuppertal, Hamburg, Leverkusen, Bremen, Innsbruck, Salzburg, Vienna, Linz, and Villach.[32] Before the two performances on December 8 in Vienna, there was also one in Kiev, on November 29, 1977.[33]

The programs on the tour consisted of Schnittke's Concerto Grosso no. 1, Pärt's *Tabula Rasa*, and a chamber music arrangement of Dmitri Shostakovich's String Quartet no. 8, as well as compositions by J. S. Bach, W. A. Mozart, and Franz Schubert (▶ audio 4.3). There were two separate programs. In the first, Schnittke's composition appeared in the second half, after the intermission. In the second program, Pärt's composition took that place, but this alternative program was performed much less frequently than the first: Sondeckis reckoned Schnittke's Concerto Grosso no. 1 was played twenty-one times, Pärt's *Tabula Rasa* only four. In the group's second concert in Vienna, in the Musikverein, both compositions appeared on the same program, with *Tabula Rasa* before the intermission and Concerto Grosso no. 1 after.[34]

In 1982, Kremer noted, "Not only the premieres in 1977 in Leningrad, Moscow, and Vilnius, but overall, everywhere we featured it on tour was a great experience."[35] Kremer remembered the performance in Stuttgart as a lone moment when the audience seemed displeased. He said "several indignant listeners left the hall during the performance and slammed the doors."[36] Despite the successes, Kremer recalled the tour as "very stressful," "for many reasons":

> I think that my decision at that time—to adopt a different position and to cross the border in such an unusual way—undoubtedly had intrigued him [Schnittke]. It was a fairly intensive trip, and he was able to meet ordinary people and fellow musicians. I remember his enthusiastic response to a meeting with Stockhausen. And I discovered later that Stockhausen was equally enthusiastic.[37]

By the "decision" and the "different position," Kremer alludes to his intent to stay in Europe, not as a defector but on an extended tour outside the Soviet Union. According to Kremer, he informed Schnittke about his "decision" on the airplane from Russia, and Schnittke reacted with understanding but also sadness.[38] Alexander Ivashkin reports that (unsubstantiated) rumors reached Moscow that Schnittke also intended to defect.[39]

For Schnittke, the tour caused anxiety on another level, at least according to Kremer. Schnittke was embarrassed by how well his Concerto Grosso no. 1 did, telling Kremer, "Success disturbs me. It's time to write something that will not be successful."[40] Elsewhere, Kremer recalled the comment differently, reporting that Schnittke said, more poetically, "It is too dangerous to ride a wave of success!"[41]

We will turn to the critical responses to the tour in the next chapter, but for now let us consider the recordings that emerged thanks to it before, during, and after. Before the tour, in mid-August 1977, Kremer and Grindenko recorded

FIGURE 4.2   Tatiana Grindenko, Gennady Rozhdestvensky, and Gidon
Kremer during the 1977 recording sessions in Vienna (detail, back
cover of Eurodisc LP SQ 25099 MK).

the Concerto Grosso no. 1 with an underrehearsed London Symphony Orchestra, conducted by Rozhdestvensky, at the Universität Salzburg between the ensemble's fourth and fifth concerts at the Salzburg Festival (figure 4.2). (The other work they recorded was Jean Sibelius's Violin Concerto, with Kremer as soloist.) According to the liner notes accompanying the Eurodisc release of this recording, "the string players of the LSO had not been able to acquaint themselves with the complicated Schnittke score until shortly before the beginning of the recording sessions."[42] During the 1977 Salzburg Festival, Kremer and Grindenko

FIGURE 4.3   Tatiana Grindenko and Gidon Kremer, *Ausgewählte Duos* cover
(Eurodisc/Melodia LP 200 083-405, 1977).

also recorded an album of duets, on which Schnittke's *Moz-Art* appeared (figure 4.3).

During the tour, on November 26, 1977, the Concerto Grosso no. 1 was recorded and filmed before a live audience of around three hundred in the studios of Bonn radio and television (WDR), along with Bach's Double Violin Concerto, Schubert's Rondo in A Major for Violin and Orchestra (with Kremer as soloist), and, as an encore of sorts, two duets by Leopold Mozart played by Kremer and Grindenko (nos. 2 and 4 of his twelve duets).[43] As he did on the tour, Schnittke played the keyboard parts; he appeared prominently on the screen, his reticent, almost frozen demeanor a complete contrast to Kremer's exuberant gymnastics. Although never officially released, these powerful, authoritative recordings were aired on both German television and radio. Schnittke's friend, East German composer Tilo Medek wrote to him in July 1978 with the news that he had heard the recording while driving in his car.[44] The score was also soon published, by Universal Edition in 1978 and by Sovetskii kompozitor in 1979, another indication of its marketability both in the Soviet Union and abroad (figure 4.4).

Kremer and Grindenko did not have a monopoly on performances, and when Kremer remained behind in Europe and the rest of the ensemble returned to the Soviet

FIGURE 4.4   Cover of Sovetskii kompozitor edition of Concerto Grosso no. 1 (detail).

Union, Grindenko quickly found a substitute: Ukrainian violinist Krysa, like Kremer a former pupil of Oistrakh's at the Moscow Conservatory. (In 1977, he became first violinist with the famous Beethoven Quartet in Moscow.) "The first time I played it," Krysa reported, "I was very nervous. After Gidon left—Grindenko invited me to play it."[45] Their first performance was in Petrozavodsk, likely in 1978 or 1979.

A few years later, in September 1983, Krysa was asked to record the Concerto Grosso no. 1 in Georgia with Liana Isakadze and her Georgian Chamber Orchestra, with Sondeckis conducting. Schnittke played the piano part, and Natalya Mandenova played the harpsichord.[46] This was the first recording of the composition made in the Soviet Union, but it was not the first released there. That honor belonged to the Eurodisc/Melodia version of the Sibelius and Schnittke pairing featuring Kremer and Grindenko with the London Symphony Orchestra and Rozhdestvensky. But the Krysa and Isakadze recording stands out as the lone commercially available example we have of Schnittke performing the piano part for his composition. Despite its many strengths, this recording did not achieve the distribution and success of the Kremer and Grindenko releases. Later reviewers overlooked it entirely.[47] Kremer and Grindenko had set the standard by cornering the market outside the Soviet Union's borders.


## IV

At the end of the Cadenza, the Butterfly cadence pivots from the gloomy disorientation of the Recitativo and the Cadenza back to the familiar. Chigaryova calls this cadential theme "one of Schnittke's best."[48] It is heard in full three times in the cartoon—at the very beginning (after a very brief title shot) and twice near its end (once at the climax of the film and once under the closing credits, where it finally resolves). The sequence at the climax of the cartoon resembles the form the cadence takes in the Concerto Grosso no. 1 between Cadenza and Rondo, with the cadence in the cartoon leading into a lush, quasi-baroque melody. It arrives at a representation of natural beauty. In the Concerto Grosso no. 1, the cadence arrives somewhere else entirely. The most blatant signal of the transformation of this cadence in the concerto grosso, beyond its transposition from G to C, is the change in mode: at the very end of *Butterfly*, the cadence resolves to major; in the Cadenza of Concerto Grosso no. 1, it resolves to the C minor of the opening chorale (⏵ video 4.1). But instead of the opening chorale, it leads directly into the initial theme of the next movement, Rondo.

## CHAPTER 5

# RONDO

After the cadence, a return to movement and melody. Canonic fragments in the soloists, waves of chords in the harpsichord underneath. Aggressive, sharply attacking, the music lingers between cooperation and conflict. Ensemble and soloists finally work together, for a time. But the stalled harpsichord figure from the introduction returns, not once but twice (mm. 33–34, rehearsal 6 in both scores; and m. 46, just before rehearsal 8/9).[1] A frenzied, repetitive episode follows. BACH in the violas and cellos pushes against the other, fragmented voices (mm. 53–70; rehearsals 9–11/10–12). The first theme returns, grooving, almost jazzy, driving to its end. But it segues seamlessly into . . . a tango. Illusion? Dream? We lose sight of the goal, trapped in the seductive present.

Back to the frantic opening, interrupted by unison hammering. Building to a close, the machinery, propulsive, obsessive, again begins to overheat, becoming ever more frantic as the end approaches. Again the cadence. Sudden clarity. Again the chorale. A deus ex machina but really a ghost in the machine (⏵ audio 5.1).

*I*

Like everything in this composition, the Rondo is constructed from a minimum of means. It opposes two related themes—the rondo theme itself (the chorus from the first song in *The Tale of the Moor of Peter the Great*) and the theme of the central tango episode. These are separated by recurrent toccata-like material. The climax of the movement arrives with the superpositioning of the rondo and tango themes, interrupted by a dual return—first of the Butterfly cadence and second of the prepared piano chorale.

The Rondo is a microcosm of the entire work. It exemplifies the polystylistic, all-but-the-kitchen-sink aesthetic contemporary reviewers often noted. The form of the movement, ABACA, is a simplified version of that found in the second movement of Schnittke's Symphony no. 1, itself based on the third, Mahler movement of Luciano Berio's *Sinfonia*. Berio did not incorporate popular music into his *Sinfonia*, but Schnittke included a jazz ensemble as a significant episode of his Symphony no. 1. In this Rondo, he did something similar: its penultimate moment, the C section, is an extended tango.

This tango presents the greatest stylistic rupture in the composition, the most extensive and most complete "other voice." As Kremer remarked, it "is also certainly a reminder of how to combine incompatible elements."[2] The reference is not transitory. It, strikingly, is a complete tango that does not stop after its initial phrases (example 5.1; ▶ audio 5.2).

EXAMPLE 5.1   Alfred Schnittke, Concerto Grosso no. 1, movement 5, Rondo, tango, measures 91–103.

Pausing before rehearsal 15/16, it quickly dives back into its own B section, a refrain. Form and, hence, time become ever more suspended. The soloists in every available recording treat the tango melody with extreme flexibility, fluidly speeding up and slowing down as the phrasing seems to suggest.

The movement back to the rondo material is equally crucial. The tango does not end abruptly. It is exaggerated and degraded in the micropolyphonic strings at rehearsal 16/17 but appears once again right before rehearsal 17/18, stripped down and attenuated, only the soloists playing pizzicato over the harpsichord, the strings nearly silent in the background (example 5.2; ▶ audio 5.3).[3]

Although this is the first prominent tango in Schnittke's output, it connects to earlier popular gestures in his music and to other contemporary trends in Soviet popular and "academic" music. "But in one sense this tango is a continuation of the *Serenade* [1968]," Kremer remarked. "And the saxophone in the Fourth Violin Concerto [1984] is a continuation of the tango. There are many things that join Alfred's works together."[4] Schnittke apparently had sung tangos at home as a child.[5] His statement about his "grandmother's favorite tango" was only partially in jest. He later recalled with some defensiveness the accusations of plagiarism that fellow composer Nikolai Karetnikov had lodged against him for the tangos in both the Concerto Grosso no. 1 and the later *Faust Cantata* (1983) (▶ audio 5.4). Karetnikov had used a tango—although not the same one—at a climactic point in his opera *Mystery of Saint Paul* (*Misteriia Apostola Pavla*, 1970–87)—the moment of Nero's suicide (▶ audio 5.5).[6] But these examples represent

EXAMPLE 5.2    Alfred Schnittke, Concerto Grosso no. 1, movement 5, Rondo,
               solo violins and harpsichord only, measures 124–30, one before
               rehearsal 17 (Universal)/ 18 (*Critical Edition*).

a larger phenomenon: the Soviet fascination with the tango
extending back to the 1920s. As Kremer noted in a brief
summary, some tangos had risen almost to the level of
folksongs in the Soviet Union.[7]

Musicologist and critic Tatiana Cherednichenko
critiqued the tango in Schnittke's *Faust Cantata*, but her
statements apply to the tango in the Concerto Grosso no. 1
as well: "If in the 1930s the tango might still have seemed
the embodiment of cultural decay, then by the 1980s, and
after punk rock, it already smelled of Victorian naïveté, it
was a nostalgic comfort for four-square, narrow-minded

people."[8] Schnittke's comment about his grandmother acknowledged as much. Rather than incendiary, the tango felt too comfortable to Cherednichenko. The disjunction, audible in the Concerto Grosso no. 1, became magnified in his *Faust Cantata*, where a tango accompanies the terrible moment when Mephistopheles collects Faust's soul. According to Cherednichenko, Schnittke meant the Mephistopheles tango "as a cultural-critical defamation of norms," but in the 1980s, it backfired on him: the tango was both "inadequately satanic" and catchy. What was intended as criticism became celebrated.[9]

## II

Tremblay refers to the significance this tango held in its source film, *Agony*, where it remained allied to Rasputin's seductive immorality. But Tremblay is not sure that it conveys this message in the concerto grosso. "It is not so immediately evident that the tango symbolizes evil," he says, "or that it acts as some sort of bait, or even that it should be seen as a negative force." He continues, "When the tango is heard in the fifth movement" of the Concerto Grosso no. 1, "it resembles more a solution than a problem." Later he calls it a "dream," as well as "the image of an unattainable goal." Yet it is also "evil in disguise."[10]

It has become a received truth that in Schnittke's music, popular themes equal evil, but this was not always the case.[11] His representational approaches had greater flexibility both within individual works and across his creative life, and his music was colored by many shades of good and evil. We do not need to tie this tango explicitly to Rasputin or the fall of the Romanovs to hear disquiet in the Rondo. Although she has called the tango the "sharpest stylistic collapse" in the composition, Savenko hears greater foreboding elsewhere in the movement.[12] "The elements of the baroque here are a power far from absolutely positive," she says. "The baroque motorics are also the most sinister rustling of enlivened marionettes, the frighteningly regular, mechanical activity of 'life's mousy fuss.'"[13] Savenko quotes here from Pushkin's well-known 1830 poem "Lines Composed at Night during Insomnia" (*Stikhi, sochinennye noch'iu vo vremia bessonnitsy*). In this poem, the speaker is tormented in the dark by unseen sounds, some quotidian, some more menacing. The speaker wonders what they all mean: "Are you calling me, or prophesizing? / I want to understand you, / I seek meaning in you." The poem's ending was long believed to be "I learn your dark language" (*Temnyi tvoi iazyk uchu*), a substitution by a friend that was thought to be Pushkin's until the 1920s. Savenko seems to be under the influence of this black close, elaborating on Pushkin's nocturnal murmurings by adding menacing marionettes, the vengeful Petrushka from the end of the Ballets Russes spectacle.

Savenko's interpretation further complicates Schnittke's own comments about the "banality" in the work, and particularly this movement. Referring to Schnittke's reference to Thomas Mann's "Tonio Kröger," she says: "And the banality, it seems, is not only a fatal power of destruction (at the climax the framing motive [the chorale] sounds like the tragic summation of the composition), but also a symbol of life, overlooked by biased tastes."[14]

Both Savenko and Kremer noted the work's indebtedness to Mann's novella. Kremer said, "In one passage the main character talks about the power of vulgarity or ordinariness in human life, and about how vulgarity and banality are not in opposition to human beings but are part of them."[15] He glosses the following passage by Mann: "It is the normal, respectable, and admirable that is the kingdom of our longing: life, in all its seductive banality."[16]

Schnittke seemed to express a similar, ambivalent interpretation of banality in some of his comments from the 1970s. To Hannelore Gerlach in 1972, he spoke about the polystylism in his Violin Sonata no. 2, *Serenade* for five musicians, and Symphony no. 1 in utopian terms:

> It is a harmonious eclecticism . . ., in which no stylistic hierarchy is conveyed, rather all styles reciprocally reveal their conventionality. And the meaning of these works lies not in the notes but in the tension of the stylistic divergences, and, consequently, between the notes.[17]

In his Russian program note for Concerto Grosso no. 1, he went further, declaring that his "lifelong task would be to bridge the gap between serious music and music for entertainment, even if I broke my neck in the process."[18] He also spoke in this note, as we have seen, about a "utopia consisting of a single style." Yet not long after, already in the early 1980s, his opinion seemed to have shifted markedly: no longer interested in bridging gaps, he again emphasized tensions. Speaking of the Concerto Grosso no. 1, a critic responded in kind: "Here there is also a tragic element, but there is also evil, blithe music. This makes the composition rich with internal contrasts."[19]

Given such equivocal instructions, how the tango in the Concerto Grosso no. 1 was actually performed became crucial for expressing its meaning. Like the tango in the *Faust Cantata*, it is a pivotal moment—and a tune that haunts the memory. But how to play it—comically or seriously, polished or raw? Kholopova said that the tango surprised its first auditors, who "already were very familiar with Schnittke's new method [of polystylism]." Now, "suddenly something impertinent and immodest came out that almost forced one to plug their ears. A typical tango you would hear in a restaurant rang out with all the vulgar phrases in its melody and the typical syncopations in the accompaniment." As in the tango's original context in *Agony*, in the Concerto Grosso no. 1 it represented a "scandal against good taste." "Yet," Kholopova noted, "when the initial shock passed, listeners already began to like the sensuous tango, and during the following performances of the concerto grosso the public always looked forward to that moment."[20]

The incongruity of the tango caused surprise. Kremer recalled that it was his first time playing a tango but that he did so "enthusiastically."[21] His enthusiasm at this moment is more than evident on the WDR television broadcast. But for Chigaryova, his fervor, and that of other performers, became too much: "What poses the performers struck and what facial expressions they made at the premiere, and also later!"[22] Oleh Krysa said, "Everyone always laughed at the tango." To counteract this response, he tried to emphasize its "delicateness, a kind of reminder that there is repose," while avoiding "making it too schmaltzy."[23] The tango was dangerous: its vulgarity threatened to overshadow the concerto grosso's already overdetermined neoclassicism.

## III

The tango was the most crowd-pleasing moment in a work that pleased many. We know from Schnittke's reports and the reports of his performers and scholars that, in general, the composition was a great success. But what did listeners and critics specifically think about the Concerto Grosso no. 1 when it was first heard in the concert halls of the Soviet Union, Eastern and Western Europe, and the United States? What did they single out for attention? Walter-Wolfgang Sparrer recalled the West German press accounts during the 1977 tour: "Then some music critics vilified this work as 'bold' and 'eclectic,' and also sometimes as an example of postmodern arbitrariness. Its impurity irritated; its blatant regressions annoyed, for example the idle neoclassical motorics in the second movement Toccata, nearly self-indulgently intensified into madness and the grotesque."[24] Savenko was not the only one to mistrust the baroque machinery of the Toccata and Rondo. Other European listeners were less subtle and more cutting in their judgments; after the performances in Vienna, an Austrian critic called it "no masterwork."[25]

In 1977, another German reviewer provided a familiar analysis of the Concerto Grosso no. 1, pointing out its three fundamental styles. In so doing, he revealed his own preconceptions about the composition: "First: stiff melodies made from frictional seconds. Second: contrived or found baroque quotations. Third: the destruction of these quotations in a dissonant, all-encompassing maelstrom. On the way to ruin a tango also arrives. Also some 'history.' In this respect it is akin to Mahler, who is also Schnittke's favorite composer from our century."[26] A reviewer in Bonn heard more specific cultural references amid the overall destruction: Russian folk music, a kind of "*Volkstümlichkeit* [folksiness] . . . reflected in the solo violin." Furthermore, "it was a typical Russian *Volkstümlichkeit* in the form of a music that, though deeply rooted in the conventional concerto style, seeks to destroy it."[27] A tango, folk tunes, destruction, and a self-conscious historical sense—for such critics, these were Schnittke's calling cards in the Concerto Grosso no. 1.

Valentin Silvestrov attended the late-November performance in Kiev by Grindenko and Kremer featuring Schnittke's composition (which he called Concerto) and Arvo Pärt's *Tabula Rasa*. In a letter from February 1978, he wrote, "Tanya and Gidon's concert went very well. It was even a big event for Kiev (and for me) and Pärt's music came off particularly well. And the most interesting thing about it was that the triumph was not just Pärt's doing, but also the sympathetic audience's—they, in listening, participated in its creation. It was co-creation—a very rare thing in our concert halls."[28] He continued, "Alfred's Concerto was a great success, but Pärt triumphed (and a very proper triumph, not a 'popular' one)."[29] Silvestrov called *Tabula Rasa* a "sonic icon," a term he and his exegetes later appropriated for his own compositions.[30] Thanks to *Tabula Rasa*, he continued, "the listeners (and me, too) departed musical space for an authentic existence that turned out to be inside each of us. Pärt's Concerto was a total window into that evening. Schnittke also had 'windows'—the beginning, 'Bach-Brahms,' the tango, and especially the ending."

Silvestrov even sent Schnittke a letter in which he conveyed his "impressions and underscored the connection between the two concertos as the (schematic) connection between 'human' and 'godly.'"[31] Schnittke was worldly, Pärt otherworldly; Pärt's music was liberating, Schnittke's mixtures remained limited by their "popular" components.

In Poland, the responses were more colorful. The music spoke a language the Polish critics understood; by this time, they already had heard many modern concerti grossi and other forms of retro music. Critic Olgierd Pisarenko called it "delicious baroque fun and virtuosity tinged with subtle irony and surreal jokes."[32] Musicologist Andrzej Chłopecki wrote: "The music spreads between nostalgia and scream, smiles through tears and pathos and heroism; it is music of almost psychedelic vision. Intimate music, in which intuitively are felt more elements of the future than the past. It is a picture of torn awareness, a tragic consciousness passing through the stage of positive disintegration toward integration into a higher level of illumination."[33] It was a kind of "contemporary romanticism" he said, one that "adopted the language of modernity to speak about matters of great importance." Journalist Bogusław Kaczyński called attention to "the extreme virtuosity of the composer, going smoothly from the contemporary to the baroque and back," as well as "the virtuosity of the pair of violinists, playing like one."[34] "Only the stylized tango and the prepared piano at the end are superfluous," he added, "as if from another, less attractive design."

The composition took some time to reach the United States. Boris Schwarz warmly greeted its American premiere on a program titled "U.S.S.R.—Unveiling the Avant-Garde" on January 17, 1981, performed by Juilliard's Continuum ensemble, directed by Joel Sachs. Schwarz noted, "New York suffers from an information gap with regard to recent trends in Moscow" but applauded the Continuum concert for helping to fill that gap. For Schwarz, Schnittke's composition was "the highlight of the . . . program":

> The Concerto Grosso is a clever mixture of styles, reaching from pseudo-Baroque to aleatory and salon music, spiced by an amusing tango episode and a fleeting reminiscence of the Tchaikovsky Violin Concerto. This wildly inventive eclecticism is tightly organized by Schnittke's creative intelligence.[35]

In his account of an all-Schnittke concert presented by the Continuum ensemble in 1982, Schwarz called the Concerto Grosso no. 1 "by far the most colorful and entertaining piece" on the program. "Again we admired the composer's ability to hold together such heterogeneous elements as Baroque, Tchaikovsky, Tango, and Modernism." Nonetheless, he added, "it must be admitted that the impact was somewhat less vivid than a year ago at the premiere, the shock value having worn off."[36] Schnittke's surprises had a short shelf life.

**IV**

In the Soviet Union, critics heard present-day concerns in the Concerto Grosso no. 1. The liner notes to the Krysa and Isakadze recording reveled in its contemporaneity. Musicologist Nadezhda Dimitriadi wrote, "from the first note to the last, the Concerto Grosso is based on internal dynamics; it captures the excitement of uninterrupted narration; and, as usual in Schnittke's music, it makes sense, through complex paradoxical emotional moods, of the pulse and occurrences of present-day human existence."[37] Polystylism succeeded here as a more accessible type of music, expressing, as Schnittke and such supporters as Savenko often noted, a sense of the "democraticness" of "the world today"—it ideally blended high and low.[38]

Yet rather than a kind of forward-looking hyper-socialist realism, later writers were more inclined to be distressed by Schnittke's stylistic clashes or to remain conflicted about their overall meaning. In 1990, Chigaryova summarized the work:

> There is no doubt as to the tragic conception of the Concerto Grosso. And all the same a feeling of hopelessness does not remain after hearing this composition. Its spiritual potential, the strength of the opposition it contains, an impulse to the beautiful, and the beauty of the very music itself, all give rise to catharsis.

Thus, she adds, "It is no coincidence that during [official] discussions of the Concerto Grosso . . . they noted that in this tragic composition there is much sunlight."[39]

Musicologist Tamara Levaya heard not sunrise but sunset. She spoke in 1985 of the "theme of the devaluation of artistic standards in our harsh century" in Schnittke's music. First appearing in his Symphony no. 1, she claimed, "It sounds still more clearly in the Concerto Grosso no. 1."[40] Mikhail Tarakanov seemed to agree. In his 1989 booklet *Soviet Music Yesterday and Today*, he stressed the "sharp confrontation of high and low in the First Concerto Grosso": "The trends of music from the baroque epoch are blended with sound patterns that are the fruit of a sensitive, refined consciousness and simultaneously with samples of exaggeratedly vulgar everyday music making (the music of the sentimental tango in the concerto's finale)."[41]

In 1991, Soviet musicologist Lyudmila Nikitina painted a simultaneously optimistic and bleak view of the composition. She underscored the "organic universality" of polystylism, the "combining in a single composition of elements of musical language from the baroque to contemporary hit songs." She believed that Schnittke's achievement was to recognize that "all of that is the language of music."[42] Nikitina's view of the egalitarian Schnittke, equitably and enthusiastically sampling styles high and low, was tempered nonetheless by her reading of the Concerto Grosso no. 1 and its crucial final moments, which we will return to in chapter 6.


## V

One telling reception document for the Concerto Grosso no. 1 has never been discussed. American-born, German-based choreographer John Neumeier (b. 1939) used the Concerto Grosso no. 1 in its entirety in the second act of his balletic treatment of Shakespeare's *Othello* with the Hamburg Ballet, which was first performed in January 1985. The other music he used included Pärt's *Tabula Rasa* (1977) and *Spiegel im Spiegel* (1978), music by Brazilian percussionist Naná Vasconcelos, Brazilian folk music, and earlier sources, including "Resonet in laudibus" by Michael Praetorius and several anonymous compositions from the fifteenth and sixteenth centuries (table 5.1).[43] (Neumeier

TABLE 5.1    Alfred Schnittke's music in John Neumeier's *Othello*.

| Act II: Cypress | |
|---|---|
| 1. Cassio's Morning Song | Anonymous: *Bonny Sweet Robin*, 16th century |
| | Anonymous: *Calleno custure me*, 16th century |
| | Alfred Schnittke: Concerto Grosso no. 1, 1977 |
| 2. Military Matters | Preludio Andante |
| 3. Distractions | Toccata Allegro |
| 4. Dialogue–Suspicion | Recitativo |
| 5. Despair | Cadenza |
| 6. Hallucinations | Rondo |
| 7. Consternation–Alienation | Postludio |
| 8. The Handkerchief Is Lost | Naná Vasconcelos: *Ondas*, 1979 |
| | Arvo Pärt, *Tabula Rasa*, 1977 |
| 9. Delusion–Disappointment–Decision | Ludus |
| 10. Murder | Silentium |

The German titles are as follows: 1. Morgenlied. Cassio; 2. Kriegsgeschäft; 3. Ablenkungen; 4. Dialog. Verdacht; 5. Verzweiflung; 6. Wahnvisionen; 7. Befremdung. Entfremdung; 8. Das Tuch ist verloren/Die Hure Bianca; 9. Täuschung. Enttäuschung. Entscheidung; 10. Mord.

Transcribed from the program books for the original Hamburg Ballet performances at the Hamburg State Opera at the Kampnagelfabrik, January 1985, 58; and for the Hamburg Ballet performances at Harris Theater, Chicago, February 2016, 3.

later said he picked Pärt's and Schnittke's compositions not knowing the link between them.)[44] The ballet quickly entered the repertory of the Hamburg Ballet, and a later high-profile performance with Kremer and Grindenko (who had not performed in the ballet's premiere) was broadcast on West German television in August 1987. It prominently featured the two violinists in the opening and closing credits and during the performance itself: once Schnittke's Concerto Grosso no. 1 starts, they appear, stealing screen time from the dancers. Yet again, the two star performers sealed their ownership of the Pärt and Schnittke compositions.[45]

A sixtieth-birthday greeting from Neumeier to Schnittke was published in the celebratory book put together by his publisher, Sikorski, in 1994.[46] Neumeier recalled, "When I first heard your Concerto Grosso, I was moved, and I had to respond with movement. This movement turned into my ballet *Othello*."[47] Curiously, at the beginning of the autograph score of the composition at Goldsmiths (Sc 010), "Otello" is written at the very top of the score's first page (following the title page), but when, by whom, and for what reason remain unclear.

Neumeier had long favored Schnittke. He once listed his ideal collaborators, his artistic "dream team," as Peter Shaffer, librettist; David Hockney, designer; and Alfred Schnittke, composer.[48] In a 1988 interview, Neumeier tied his musical choices for *Othello*'s score to the basic "confusion" of the plot, two lovers (Desdemona and Othello) muddled by a third (Iago): "Therefore as a foundation I have always wanted very enervating, quasi-deconstructed music." He had originally planned for an entirely new score to accompany his interpretation, but when this idea "disintegrated," he "very quickly decided to surround Alfred Schnittke's Concerto Grosso [no. 1] with the most varied compositions. In this work I was then fascinated by the contrasts—but also the correspondences—between so-called old and so-called new music."[49] "In connection with scenery and movement a Renaissance song can appear modern," he said, "and together with traditional pieces a contemporary composition gains comparable precision and force."[50]

For Neumeier, Schnittke's and Pärt's music evoked the "interior landscape" of the characters in the second half.[51] Schnittke's Toccata in particular served as an ideal background for the growing strain between Iago and Othello in the section he called "Distractions." At the anxious climax of the movement, Iago pulls Desdemona away, boosted by the Toccata's mounting tension and freneticism (▶ video 5.1).[52] Pärt's *Tabula Rasa*, by contrast, accompanied Othello's murder of Desdemona. Neumeier's other titles suggest an intriguing reading of Schnittke's Concerto Grosso no. 1. The Cadenza underscores Othello's anguish in a scene called "Despair," and "Dialogue–Suspicion" matches the ambiguities in the Recitativo, the soloists' strange relationship both to each other and to the ensemble. Hearing the Rondo as hallucinatory also captures its mix of tones and styles, even as it ties this moment in Schnittke's output to other collage forebears, chief among them George Rochberg's *Music for the Magic Theater* (1965), itself based on a hallucinatory episode from Hermann Hesse's 1927 novel *Steppenwolf*.[53]

Although the reviews were decidedly mixed, most critics discussed the music in Neumeier's production.[54] In notes she made during the premiere performance, American costume designer Marna King wrote that a friend "says he [Neumeier] can create incredible images but that he knows nothing about music. Some comment that it all seems the same after so many pieces."[55] Wolfgang Willaschek highlighted the "affinities" between Pärt's and Schnittke's compositions, particularly their "unacademic manner." But he also noted their differences: "In Schnittke one can hear how apparently 'baroque' music is nearly destroyed over and over again through contemporary compositional methods, and with Pärt one finds a sonic sensuousness reminiscent of 'minimal music' that recalls music from a forgotten time."[56]

In a preview article published before the premiere, the *Hamburger Abendblatt* interviewed the concertmaster of the Hamburger Symphoniker, Janos Hörömpö, who performed as one of the soloists in both *Tabula Rasa* and Concerto Grosso no. 1. He surprisingly declared the two works "incomprehensible." Rather than the emotions, Hörömpö said, "One can cope with such constructed works only with the intellect. I resolved to deal with Schnittke's music as if it were an étude." Hörömpö also complained that his work on the ballet's score had brought him only "anger and aggressions." Nonetheless, he admitted, "It's not so bad for the orchestra. They need to learn a couple of wrong notes and rhythmic finesse."[57] Despite these grumbles, the performance impressed others. One critic was so overwhelmed by the "vivid" playing of the musicians that he "was temporarily (and illicitly) disposed to pay more attention to them than to the choreography on the stage."[58]

Neumeier had originally been inspired by the motion he sensed in Schnittke's score, a sensation perhaps grounded by the music's origin in film music, and many dancers remain fascinated by its intertwined kinesthetic and narrative possibilities. Kholopova remarked on the popularity of the Concerto Grosso no. 1 for dancers: "In Russian ballet classes, this composition became just as popular as the waltzes from Tchaikovsky's ballets."[59] It has become popular not just in Russia: in 2005 and 2014, it served as part of the score for *Dracula*, presented by the Northern Ballet Theatre in England; and in 2017 and 2018, no fewer than three ballets performed across Europe used the Concerto Grosso no. 1 as part of their scores: *Anne Frank* (Karlsruhe, Germany), *Medea* (Tallinn, Estonia), and *Don Quichotte* (Flensburg, Germany).[60]

In Schnittke's score, motion and movement prove erratic. Just as quickly as dynamism begins, it abruptly ceases. The Rondo starts and stops, halts and hovers; herky-jerky, it traverses a wide emotional compass. It reaches prematurely the now-known cadence, a final moment before the final movement actually begins. The familiar chorale thunders back. Although traversed, the abyss still gapes.

## CHAPTER 6

# POSTLUDIO

A MID SHARDS OF SILENCE, glimmers. The violins are rendered nearly speechless. Like characters from Samuel Beckett, they mutely eke out scraps of previous melodies, now relegated to the edges of their upper registers. The opening figuration is a reprise of the violin entrance in the Preludio, itself reprised in the Cadenza's opening. The Preludio's suspended time returns. Other wisps of previous music come back in the accompanying ensemble, particularly the first Toccata theme, now at the blurry boundary of audibility.

The conclusion includes very little material; even the cluster held by the strings can be interpreted as supersaturated micropolyphony—simultaneous echoes. The first fourteen measures in the violins are almost exactly the same as their initial entrance in the Preludio; a few notes are altered, and instead of playing without vibrato, the violins now sound harmonics. From measures 10 to 15, the piano tolls a repeated C in its depths, an (unprepared) pitch accompanied in the (prepared) right hand by tolling fourths (D–G–C#), onto which another fourth is slowly superimposed: F# is added in measure 12 and a B♮ in measure 15. The piano strokes here are particularly harsh in Schnittke's performance on Krysa and Isakadze's recording—lightning strikes in the dark.

In measure 15, the solo violins disintegrate in a quasi-improvisatory downward slide. At the comparable moment in the Preludio, they had begun their first extended duet. But the time for duets has passed. Instead, three bars from the Toccata's main theme recur, pianississimo (*ppp*), starting on A—implying A minor but also with tendencies to C major. The flickering quotation is broken off abruptly in measure 19 by more bell tolling in the prepared piano, again over C in the depths.

There exist several variants for this piano sonority. Although it is consistently grounded on D, Schnittke changed the last piano chord several times. In the early full scores at Goldsmiths, it contains nine pitches, and in the first published editions, it contains two clusters, one spanning D to A♭ in the left hand the other B to D# in the right. The critical edition includes a version containing six pitches (two superimposed inverted triads: D–F#–B and E#–G–C#) found in yet another score in the composer's hand.[1] Schnittke perhaps experimented with these variations as much for their sound on the prepared piano as for their harmonic implications. For any of the possible harmonies he tested theoretically could resolve almost anywhere. But they actually resolve nowhere—to the attenuated, coded cluster in the solo violins that follows, C–B–A–B♭, and the lone, tolling C (▶ audio 6.1).

*I*

Although Lyudmila Nikitina discerned hope in Schnittke's Concerto Grosso no. 1, she ultimately rendered it in disheartening hues, comparing it to director Andrei Tarkovsky's 1979 film *Stalker* and the 1986 postapocalyptic Soviet film *Letters from a Dead Man* (*Pis'ma mertvogo cheloveka*, dir. Konstantin Lopushansky). She heard the destruction of a civilization in the concerto grosso's many barren stretches, its fragmented distortions of past practices, and its ending. The final movement of the Concerto Grosso no. 1 "is like an oblique view of a great civilization from which only twisted fragments remain," she wrote, "like after a universal catastrophe" (▶ video 6.1).[2] (The composer of the score for *Letters from a Dead Man* is slightly incongruous: Alexander Zhurbin, better known as the author of the pioneering Soviet rock opera *Orpheus and Eurydice* from 1975.)[3]

Elsewhere, Nikitina recalled a more specific filmic moment. "The image of destroyed civilization is somewhat reminiscent of a scene from Tarkovsky's *Stalker*," she wrote, "shreds of paper floating in pools of water." Overall, Nikitina found that the concerto grosso's "tragic sense of time . . . approached the tense atmosphere of the atomic age, with the threat of atomic catastrophe hanging over humanity."[4] Svetlana Savenko's "enlivened marionette" took on even more unsettling connotations: everyday individuals suspended helplessly beneath the threat of nuclear apocalypse, pawns in a geopolitical game.

Yet Nikitina translates the work too harshly. Pursuing her references proves instructive. There actually are three moments in *Stalker* in which papers appear submerged in water. All are in the second section of the film, when Stalker and the men he is guiding in the mysterious Zone, Writer and Professor, grow closer to their destination—a room they hope will fulfill their deepest desires—yet become more and more weary and apprehensive about their goal. The briefest glimpse of paper occurs at 1:20:36–1:20:46, just after the trio debates the meaning and existence of happiness. The camera pans down from a shot of Stalker's head, and for ten seconds we focus on a gold object of some sort. A bullet? A vial? Next to this object are scraps of paper with print on them, illegible (▶ video 6.2).

The other two moments bracket this one. The next-longest sight of paper in water precedes it, occurring near the end of the tracking shot from 1:13:30–1:14:06 as Stalker and Writer lose Professor and pass through the ironically named "dry tunnel," a tortuous cavern buffeted by surging cascades of water. Having traversed this obstacle, they walk past inexplicably glowing coals, and the camera pans from the coals to a shallow pool with cracked tiles and drowned debris, including syringes and guns, concluding with a brief glimpse of calendar pages in the water. They emerge in the next cut to find Professor inexplicably back where they had started (▶ video 6.3).

The final, longest moment of paper submerged in water occurs from 1:24:38–1:28:02. After their befuddling journey through the "dry tunnel," the three men rest. As Stalker lies on an islet of moss in a stagnant body of water, an iconic image from the film, the camera again tracks over submerged tiles, now vertically. We see many of the same objects from the initial tracking shot after the "dry tunnel" but in slower, more languorous detail: syringes, guns, tools, fish in a rocking bowl, religious iconography (from Jan van Eyck's Ghent altarpiece), coins, a spring, and, again, a calendar page, marked 28 (the earlier calendar pages were 27 and 29, of an unknown month) (1:27:08). Then we return to the submerged hand of the sleeping Stalker. Both this and the previous moment (1:13:00–1:14:00) signal time's fluidity—in both, we arrive back where we started. To heighten the (illusory) sense of time ending, the second tracking shot is accompanied by a woman's voice whispering from the Book of Revelation (6:12–17), succeeded by atmospheric synthesizer music by Eduard Artyemev (the composer of the soundtrack) (▶ video 6.4).[5]

Like Tarkovsky's earlier film *Solaris* (1972), *Stalker* concerns faith and the unknown, outer and inner dreams. It is a journey into an abandoned, mysteriously altered past by protagonists hoping for a better future. Nikitina focused only on the destruction, but Tarkovsky wanted the film to be about hope, and his critics agreed.[6] "Actually, this story is about the crisis of one of the world's last remaining idealists," Tarkovsky said.[7] He rejected the idea that the film was "despairing," echoing the official commentary about Schnittke's Concerto Grosso no. 1 cited by Chigaryova (and the larger Soviet emphasis on "optimistic tragedy"). "Even if it contains moments of despair," Tarkovsky argued, "it still rises above them. It's a sort of catharsis. It's a tragedy and a tragedy isn't despairing. It's a story of destruction, which leaves the viewer with a sense of hope, because of the catharsis that Aristotle describes. Tragedy purifies man."[8] For the entirety of the film, it remains unclear whether Stalker is bluffing—whether there really are unexplained forces in the Zone. Although they are given glimpses, Professor and Writer never find out.

The conclusion to the film reveals the truth. Back in Stalker's run-down lodging, his daughter, named Monkey, somehow, without physically touching it, causes two glasses and a jar to move across a table. Critic Geoff Dyer calls it "one of the all-redeeming moments of any art form."[9] Yet it is a strange, ambivalent gesture. In an unexpected way, change has happened: the mind has an impact on the world. Was this Stalker's wish, warped? "From a symbolic point of view," Tarkovsky said, Monkey's mysterious powers "represent new perspectives, new spiritual powers that are as yet unknown to us, as well as new physical forces."[10] He also admitted: "I don't know about the little girl, . . . She represents hope, quite simply" (▶ video 6.5).[11]

**II**

The Postludio to the Concerto Grosso no. 1 plays a central role in an unusual late-Soviet pairing of Vladimir Vysotsky and Schnittke, a pairing no doubt based on their previous work together in Alexander Mitta's *The Tale of the Moor of Peter the Great* but also on their work at Moscow's Taganka

Theater. Alexander Ivashkin once suggested to Schnittke that director Larisa Shepitko was "more cultured" than Vysotsky. "I beg to differ!," Schnittke responded. "Vysotsky was much more cultured than the character in his songs. After all, that character, that guy—that's not Vysotsky. Vysotsky was Hamlet: he understood and felt all of that."[12] One of Vysotsky's most famous roles had indeed been Hamlet; his rendition of "To be, or not to be" became legendary (▶ audio 6.2).

Schnittke and Vysotsky were joined in a posthumous album of Vysotsky's ballads (*ballady*) from 1990 called *About Time and Fate* (*O vremeni i o sud'be*) recited by actress Antonina Kuznetsova (b. 1941) (figure 6.1).[13] (Vysotsky

FIGURE 6.1   Vladimir Vysotsky, *About Time and Fate: Ballads* (Melodiia LP S40-29415-001, 1990).

died in 1980 at the age of forty-two.) Although most of the album consists of Kuznetsova's unaccompanied readings of Vysotsky's poetry, Schnittke's music serves as introduction, transition, and occasional formal marker within each poem. The selections are drawn from two compositions: his *Two Little Pieces for Organ* from 1980, performed by Oleg Yanchenko, and the Concerto Grosso no. 1, performed by Gidon Kremer and Tatiana Grindenko.[14] The entire album begins with chords from the organ composition, but the Concerto Grosso no. 1 plays a greater role. The second side of the LP starts with the reappearance of the prepared piano chorale at the end of the Rondo, introducing Vysotsky's "History of an Illness" (*Istoriia bolezni*) before fading away.

During the last selections of side 2, the Concerto Grosso no. 1 is heard more frequently. The prepared piano melody from the Rondo softly slips into the penultimate poem, the "Ballad of the Abandoned Ship" (*Ballada o broshennom korable*).[15] From this moment until the end, the remainder of Concerto Grosso no. 1 is heard in full. The final poem, "There Is Ice Below and Above" (1980), Vysotsky's last, dedicated to his wife, Marina Vlady, overlays most of Schnittke's Postludio (figure 6.2).[16] There is even (possibly intentional) word painting: the final two lines of the poem—"I have something to sing, to present before the almighty, / I have something with which to justify myself before him"—sound over the echoed recollection of the Toccata theme in Schnittke's work (⊙ audio 6.3).

Vladimir Vysotsky, "There Is Ice Below and Above" (*I snizu led, i sverkhu*), 1980, translation by Peter Schmelz.

| | |
|---|---|
| И снизу лед, и сверху. Маюсь между. | There is ice below and above. I suffer in between. |
| Пробить ли верх иль пробуравить низ? | Should I break through above or drill down below? |
| Конечно, всплыть и не терять надежду, | Of course, float to the top without losing hope, |
| А там - за дело в ожиданьи виз. | and there the matter of awaiting authorization. |
| Лед надо мною, надломись и тресни! | Ice above me, fracture and crack! |
| Я весь в поту, как пахарь от сохи. | I am drenched in sweat, like a plowman from his labor. |
| Вернусь к тебе, как корабли из песни, | I will return to you, like the ship from the song, |
| Все помня, даже старые стихи. | Recalling everything, even the old verses. |
| Мне меньше полувека - сорок с лишним, | I am less than a half-century old— forty plus change, |
| Я жив, двенадцать лет тобой и господом храним. | I am alive, twelve years thanks to you and the Lord. |
| Мне есть что спеть, представ перед всевышним, | I have something to sing, to present before the almighty, |
| Мне есть чем оправдаться перед ним. | I have something with which to justify myself before him. |

The icy entrapment of Vysotsky's poem matches the icy boundaries of *Stalker*. As they approach their final destination in the film, the characters pass through an ice-encrusted tunnel nicknamed the "meat grinder." It is the last obstacle before the promised final salvation of the room. Water in all its forms surrounds and penetrates the film.

FIGURE 6.2    Vladimir Vysotsky and Marina Vlady in 1979. Sovfoto/UIG/
Bridgeman Images. Used with permission.

In freezing, water kills, but it also preserves—entombing
the past, promising future salvation. From this perspec-
tive, Schnittke's Concerto Grosso no. 1 enacts memory and
nostalgia, entrapment and preservation. When paired with
Vysotsky's valedictory poem, its recollected melodies signal
not destruction but redemption, paralleling the anticipated
redemption of the room in *Stalker*.

### III

The Concerto Grosso no. 1 is a work of echoes: between soloists, between soloists and ensemble, between

movements, between present and past, between it and other works of art—ballet, film, poetry. Savenko is right: it is tautly constructed both motivically and intonationally.[17] But these echoes and this tight integration have a downside: in the end, only undifferentiated aural fallout remains. The Concerto Grosso no. 1 unleashed a deluge of pessimistic responses. Nikitina and the producers of the Vysotsky LP were part of a larger trend already apparent in John Neumeier's *Othello* ballet that concentrated on what Tiedman called the concerto's "nightmarish or surreal distortion of familiar baroque soundworlds."[18]

In 2004, German director Volker Schlöndorff chose Schnittke's music for his film *The Ninth Day* (*Der Neunte Tag*, 2004) about a Catholic priest's incarceration at the Dachau concentration camp (figure 6.3). Schlöndorff uses the tensest music, from Recitativo, during the opening shots of the prisoners entering the camp; this is the movement from the Concerto Grosso no. 1 that he turns to most often. (He also employs excerpts from Schnittke's Cello Concerto no. 1.) Schlöndorff declared:

> This is the first time that I have made use of existing compositions in my work. I could not conceive of anyone, whether Hans-Werner Henze or someone else, writing music for this film. But ever since my last visit to St. Petersburg twelve years ago I have been carrying around a CD of Schnittke's concerto. I do not know whether, consciously or unconsciously, playing it has influenced me but there is some affinity there in that the music suits the film so extraordinarily well. This is music with a highly humanistic language. Alfred Schnittke was a lone warrior.[19]

FIGURE 6.3   *The Ninth Day* soundtrack (BIS-CD-1507, 2004).

Schlöndorff points to the inherent visuality (and hence narrativity) of Schnittke's music: "The origin of the music [in
Schnittke's film music] partly explains why it fits so well
with cinematic images. I would prefer to say nothing of the
film except: 'Listen to the music, and you will know what
the film is about!'"[20] The music is picturesque, but, more
than that, in this context it sets an almost incontrovertible
mood of gloom and despair.

The Concerto Grosso no. 1 continues to haunt. A Boston-
based ensemble called A Far Cry took this affect literally in
2009, programming Schnittke's Concerto Grosso no. 1 in
a concert the night before Halloween titled "The Lunatic,"
which also featured Heinrich Biber's "Battalia á 10";

Francesco Geminiani's Concerto Grosso no. 3; Christopher Hossfeld's "concerto GROSSO" for eighteen strings (the second movement of which is called loudly, in all capital letters, ". . . AND ZOMBIES"); and Schnittke's Concerto Grosso no. 1. A reviewer ran with the theme:

> Here, in effect, was a real zombie: At times Schnittke's piece acts like an ordinary Baroque concerto, but before long the human exterior falls away, replaced by something eerie and disturbing. Dark, atonal harmonies pile up, a tango breaks out in the harpsichord, and the music builds to fever pitches of intensity. At the end the music seems to collapse under the weight of its metamorphoses, leaving only the bleak fragments of its former self.[21]

A "Passion Concert" in Aachen, Germany, in 1989 responded to similar themes in the composition. It paired the Concerto Grosso no. 1 with Joseph Haydn's *Seven Last Words of Christ* as two works representing suffering, death, and resurrection.[22]

Many reactions to the Concerto Grosso no. 1 have, almost since its inception, tilted toward the macabre, the grim, the ghastly—the human struggle with aging and death, phantom marionettes, postnuclear apocalypse, alien "zones," and, more recently, the holocaust, vampires, and zombies. The range of references tells us something about the composition's emotional resonance. It also tells us about the status of avant-garde classical music today, best suited for science fiction and horror, the monstrously monumental.[23]

Is it any wonder that not one but two Swedish heavy metal groups, Ofermod and Ondskapt, launched records in the early 2000s with extended samples of Schnittke's music? They chose not the Concerto Grosso no. 1 but his *Faust Cantata* and Requiem, respectively (▶ audio 6.4). (The albums are Ofermod, *Mystérion tés anomias*, 1998/2005, and Ondskapt, *Draco Sit Mihi Dux*, 2003.)

Schnittke's music is also featured in other ghoulish compilations. A 2011 Naxos digital sampler called *Music for the Zombie Apocalypse* includes the first movement of Schnittke's Piano Quintet alongside disturbing (often funereal) music by Krzysztof Penderecki, Henryk Górecki, and Arvo Pärt (*Collage on the Theme BACH*), as well as by Beethoven, Mozart, and Cherubini.[24] The collection proved popular enough to justify a sequel the next year, *Music for the Zombie Apocalypse Vol. 2*, which contained Schnittke's *Stille Musik* for violin and cello from 1979. And the soundtrack for Martin Scorsese's 2010 psychological thriller *Shutter Island* placed Schnittke's *Hymn* no. 2 amid a diverse array of late-twentieth- and early-twenty-first-century music by John Cage, Nam June Paik, Morton Feldman, Penderecki, and György Ligeti.

Yet the uncanny was felt most strongly in the Concerto Grosso no. 1, in which Schnittke seemed to be resurrecting the dead—dead themes, dead genres—leading to unsettling questions about his own hand as author. When playing so obviously with antiquated (even deceased) material, who becomes the marionette and who the puppeteer? As he ceded his compositional voice to others, was the music—in some perverse, impossible sense—now playing Schnittke? Had it taken on a life of its own? What does it mean for polystylism that it is roundly heard as frightening? I asked Oleh Krysa about the meaning of the Postludio, whether it was tragic or hopeful. He emphasized its "philosophical content" and said, "It contains all the emotions: wisdom, sadness, the question of questions."[25]

Polystylism is slippery. Approached from multiple angles, it suggests multiple interpretations. Despite Schnittke's goal of a utopian blending, his wish for synthesis rather than (or as much as) "collisions," it proved (and continues to prove) a moving target, impossible to pin down.[26] Although bleak, even desperate, the critical and artistic responses point to a richer understanding of the Concerto Grosso no. 1: a sense of hope and redemption sequestered behind its tragic, often icy façade.

## IV

Unlike Pärt, Schnittke suffered few ill effects from the late-1977 tour. In 1980, Pärt left Estonia for Austria and then West Germany (albeit illegally: he ostensibly was headed to Israel because his wife was Jewish). Schnittke remained behind. He had been emotionally affected during the tour's stop in Linz, Austria, when he visited the St. Florian Monastery, site of composer Anton Bruckner's grave. Shortly afterward, Schnittke wrote his Symphony no. 2, "St. Florian," for chamber choir and orchestra (1979), a drastic stylistic shift in that it propounded only a single, overly earnest style. Discerning any irony here proved challenging. Whether a result of the 1977 tour or a Cold War spat between the Soviet Union and the United Kingdom, in April 1980 Schnittke was unable to attend the symphony's premiere performances in London.[27] He was permitted to go to East Germany for the November 1981 premiere of his Symphony no. 3, dedicated to the Leipzig Gewandhaus Orchestra, but travel, particularly to Western Europe, remained a tool with which the Soviet authorities attempted to control him until the late 1980s, when his fame and the weakening strictures of the Soviet system coincided and he was allowed to go more or less wherever he pleased.[28]

Despite professing to be ashamed of the success he gained from the Concerto Grosso no. 1, Schnittke very soon wrote another. He seems to have felt as attached to the concerto grosso as a genre, an approach, and a style as he did to the symphony. He composed eight symphonies (and an unfinished, contested ninth) and six concerti grossi (table 6.1). The most he composed in any other genre was four string quartets, although he also wrote three piano sonatas and three violin sonatas, three operas (*Life with*

TABLE 6.1    Alfred Schnittke, symphonies and concerti grossi (in order of composition).

| | |
|---|---|
| Symphony no. 1 (1972) | |
| | Concerto Grosso no. 1 (1977) |
| Symphony no. 2, "St. Florian" (1979) | |
| Symphony no. 3 (1981) | |
| | Concerto Grosso no. 2 (1981–82) |
| Symphony no. 4 (1984) | |
| | Concerto Grosso no. 3 (1985) |
| Concerto Grosso no. 4/Symphony no. 5 (1988) | |
| | Concerto Grosso no. 5 (1991) |
| Symphony no. 6 (1992) | |
| Symphony no. 7 (1993) | Concerto Grosso no. 6 (1993) |
| Symphony no. 8 (1994) | |
| Symphony no. 9 (1998, unfinished) | |

*an Idiot* [1990–91], *Gesualdo* [1994], and the *History of Doctor Johann Faust* [1994]), and three ballets (*Labyrinths* [*Labirinty*, 1971], *Sketches* [*Eskizy*, 1985], and *Peer Gynt* [1986]).

Krysa remarked that each of the concerti grossi seemed to have been "written by a different composer."[29] Beyond their common use of the harpsichord, which appears in all but no. 6, they differ markedly in form and approach. Significantly, in a clear signal of his move away from the overt polystylistic dramaturgy of the 1970s, in Schnittke's subsequent concerti grossi, he never used anything but tempo indications to label the movements. By contrast, as we have seen, every movement in the Concerto Grosso no. 1 carries a generic indication: Preludio, Toccata, Recitativo, Cadenza, Rondo, Postludio. (A precursor, written just on the cusp of his first polystylistic experiments, is Schnittke's String Quartet no. 1, whose three movements are titled Sonata, Canon, and Cadenza.)

The Concerto Grosso no. 2 (1981–82) and Concerto Grosso no. 3 (1985) are closest in style and affect to the Concerto Grosso no. 1. The Concerto Grosso no. 2 draws on popular music both directly and obliquely: it opens with the solo cello and violin solemnly intoning "Silent Night"—perhaps taking a cue from the string of "Christmas" concerti grossi in the seventeenth and eighteenth centuries by Arcangelo Corelli, Pietro Locatelli, Giuseppe Torelli, and Francesco Manfredini. But then the ensemble enters, and rock music bursts in, especially in performances conducted by Gennady Rozhdestvensky. The score includes both electric and bass guitars and a battery of percussion, among which are high-hat cymbals and bongos.

Schnittke described the course of Concerto Grosso no. 3, written for two violins, harpsichord, and fourteen strings, and dedicated to five composers with notable anniversaries in 1985 (Heinrich Schütz, J. S. Bach, George Frideric Handel, Domenico Scarlatti, and Alban Berg). "It begins 'beautifully,' neoclassically," he said, "but after some minutes the museum explodes and we stand with the fragments of the past (quotations) before the dangerous and uncertain present."[30] It was a more forthright, if not fatalistic, description of the impulses behind his polystylism from Symphony no. 1 onward. Cooperation had dissipated. Now only conflict, danger, and uncertainty remained. Yet the ending of the work is magical—a recurrence of the main theme from the first movement in iridescent strings, undergirded by comforting, clockwork pizzicato, surrounded by a halo of celesta and chimes.

The Concerto Grosso no. 4 signaled a turning point. In 1985, Schnittke suffered a debilitating stroke. He claimed it, justifiably, as a key dividing point in his life, after which he claimed to feel musical form and time differently. He also spoke more openly about what he called "shadow sounds," stressing further the Neoplatonic aesthetics he had first broached in his micropolyphony essay in the early 1970s and hinted at with his sketched reference to "Peter Schlemiel." The Concerto Grosso no. 4 reveals a hybridity absent from his other essays in the genre. He combined it in a single work with his Symphony no. 5, a neat way to sidestep the Beethovenian challenge of a Fifth Symphony. He called it Concerto Grosso no. 4/Symphony no. 5 (1988). Movement 1 was a brash, almost cartoonishly bombastic, and often Stravinskian concerto grosso; its kaleidoscopic swirl of solo and ensemble instruments lacks any clear division between *concertino* and *ripieno*. It is one of his most memorable movements. The remaining three movements constitute the symphony and are based on an unfinished Gustav Mahler piano quartet fragment.[31] Schnittke remained fixated on incomplete works by past masters—primarily Mozart and Mahler. He wanted to bring them up to date by bridging the temporal gaps they represented. Or he wanted to throw into greater relief the temporal gaps between past and present. Or both. The ambiguous approach was another way for Schnittke to assert his role as author, dependent on yet master of the tradition.

In Concerto Grosso no. 5 and no. 6, baroque elements become even more tangential, despite Schnittke's claim that with no. 5 (1991), he updated Antonio Vivaldi's *Four Seasons*. The much more abstract and diffuse no. 5—for solo violin, an "invisible piano," and orchestra—is a strange amalgam of Schnittke old and new.[32] Its final movement is all shade and echo.

At less than fifteen minutes long, the three-movement Concerto Grosso no. 6 (1993) for violin, piano, and string orchestra is the shortest, most subdued of Schnittke's concerti grossi. Unlike other Schnittke compositions, it ends without culmination or apotheosis: the crashing piano chords from the lively, extroversive first movement return, answered by a distressed violin upsurge and the ensemble strings. But all are suddenly cut off, unresolved. It is a condensation of the First Concerto Grosso's Postludio, but here the return conveys only unease. (In 1986, Schnittke also arranged the Concerto Grosso no. 1 for flute, oboe, harpsichord, piano, and chamber orchestra.)[33]

Aside from the Concerto Grosso no. 2 and no. 4, the closest companion in Schnittke's output to the Concerto Grosso no. 1 is his Violin Concerto no. 4 (1984), which begins with a similar chorale and includes similar, if even more exaggerated, moments of breakdown, particularly in Krysa's powerful renderings.[34] The issue of banality became more heightened for Schnittke: he called the self-consciously "pretty" melodies in the violin concerto "painted corpses," a grisly image showing his anxiety about traditional songfulness.[35] And in this composition, he actually used Kremer's initials, in two forms: G–C–D–E (G-i-DO-n k-RE-m-E-r) and G–D–E–E (G-i-D-on kr-E-m-E-r) (▶ audio 6.5).

**V**

Recently, musicologist Ulrike Böhmer asked sixty-nine contemporary German-speaking composers their opinions about Schnittke and his music. Among the works by Schnittke that her respondents mentioned, the Concerto Grosso no. 1 stands out. The only other work mentioned as frequently was his opera *Life with an Idiot*.[36]

In Russia, Schnittke's music has retained its luster. In 2010, the magazine *Komsomol'skaia pravda* released a Schnittke disc and a lengthy booklet as the eighth part of its series of "Great Composers" (figure 6.4). The CD contained the entire *Faust Cantata*, the Rondo from Concerto Grosso no. 1, *Suite in the Old Style*, and the *Inspector General Suite* (*Revizskaia skazka*).[37] Schnittke's Concerto Grosso no. 1 also appeared on a 2015 list of "100 Compositions with Which to Start Listening to Classical Music" presented by

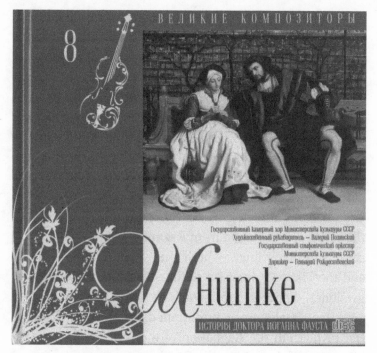

ВЕЛИКИЕ КОМПОЗИТОРЫ

8

Государственный камерный хор Министерства культуры СССР
Художественный руководитель – Валерий Полянский
Государственный симфонический оркестр
Министерства культуры СССР
Дирижёр – Геннадий Рождественский

*Шнитке*

ИСТОРИЯ ДОКТОРА ИОГАННА ФАУСТА

FIGURE 6.4   Alfred Schnittke volume in *Komsomol'skaia pravda*'s Great
Composers series (2010).

the influential magazine/website *Afisha*.[38] Two other well-known works by Schnittke also made the cut: the *Inspector General Suite* and the *Faust Cantata*. These choices privilege Schnittke the crowd pleaser—tangos and madcap marches—over his pensive, brooding side.

I recently had a lively conversation with a group of Russians about the Concerto Grosso no. 1 and about Schnittke in general. They expressed fondness but also a certain dismissiveness. Concerto Grosso no. 1 represented the past for them. It is a time capsule, caught in the cold grip of the 1980s. They heard too much "irony through perversion" in it and now find the tango and the "demonstration of evil" at its outset excessive. There is too much "doubleness" to the work, too much subtext. For them, Schnittke is connected indelibly to the 1980s—communal apartments, Soviet circumstances, the yearning for alternative narratives—and in this last respect connected to Dmitri Shostakovich. All of this restricts Schnittke, making him a relic of that decade.

The best evidence of Schnittke's role in the 1980s is the prominent placement of the Concerto Grosso no. 1 in the glasnost film *Black Square* (*Chernyi kvadrat*) from 1988, a documentary directed by Joseph Pasternak that surveys the visual arts in Russia from Kazimir Malevich to the present. Schnittke's music—both the Concerto Grosso no. 1 and the Piano Quintet (in both its original and orchestral versions)—appears throughout the film. But the Concerto Grosso no. 1 takes on an important dramatic role at the central pivot from the stagnation of the 1970s to the gradual liberation of the 1980s. The Rondo underscores a glimpse at 32:00 of the studio of artist Vadim Sidur (1924–86), a motley assortment of his figurative sculptures as well as more abstract assemblages: old bicycle tires, ladders, signs, and other odds and ends, a reflection of the repression and resistance of the 1970s (⊙ video 6.6).

This moment had been prepared by comments from poet Yunna Morits (b. 1937), who quoted Sidur's declaration that the 1970s was the "epoch of the equilibrium of fear" (31:45). Fittingly, in the documentary, during the Rondo's climactic chorale (34:10–22), the images shift to a pile of dolls (and doll parts), a horror archetype intensified by Schnittke's eerie music. Filmmakers seem unable to resist his recapitulation's harrowing affect. A voice-over from Morits

enters at 34:23 to heighten the stakes—it was a battle between good and evil in the Soviet Union, she says: "I believe
that when evil definitively won, and everyone recognized
that it was impossible to continue in this way, that everyone
had grown sick of this disgusting life, only then did good
win and the epoch of perestroika begin. But it was not that
good triumphed over evil, but that evil won out in every
aspect of our life and it became impossible to live."[39] With
the ringing of a bell, the soundtrack abruptly changes, and
another sonic icon of glasnost reverberates: the rock group
Nautilius Pompilius's anthem "Bound by a Single Chain"
(*Skovannye odnoi tsep'iu*, 1986). Schnittke and rock together became aural signals of the momentous upheavals
of the 1980s. Pasternak points to another interpretation of
the disquiet heard by many in the Concerto Grosso no. 1: it
condensed the evil of stagnation and of repression but also
the struggle against those evils.

Russian composer Viktor Yekimovsky (b. 1947) declared
that Schnittke's output was "closely tied to the era, to its
time": "It's not abstract music, it's connected to its time."
But, he admitted in 2008, "now, it doesn't work." Unlike
my other Russian interlocutors, Yekimovsky acknowledged
Concerto Grosso no. 1 as an exception, "a brilliant composition, simply magnificent," counting it among the "handful
of Schnittke's works" that still "come across as interesting,
sound good, like they did before." And the others? "They've
stopped working."[40]

More recently, Schnittke's Concerto Grosso no. 1 was
enlisted by Russian officials as a marker of "Russianness"
during the opening ceremonies of the 2014 Sochi Winter
Olympic Games. The imagery was not subtle. The Rondo

accompanied the collapse of the Russian Empire leading up to the 1917 Revolution, represented by the late stages of a grand ball with frantic groupings of dancers, strobe lights, and a snowstorm, followed by a final breakdown, giving way to a roaring oncoming train.[41] Schnittke's life-long struggle with his identity was increasingly resolved by others toward the Russian side, a process that began with his burial in Moscow's Novodevichy Cemetery (figure 6.5).

FIGURE 6.5    Alfred Schnittke's tombstone, Novodevichy Cemetery, Moscow. Photo © Peter Schmelz.

ALFRED SCHNITTKE'S CONCERTO GROSSO NO. 1

The appearance of Concerto Grosso no. 1 in Sochi as a signal of a collapsing civilization—a variation on its role in the *Black Square* documentary—offers yet another twist on the composition's malevolence.

How does Schnittke's Concerto Grosso no. 1 sound near the end of the second decade of the twentieth-first century elsewhere? For many, he has been superseded. Tim Rutherford-Johnson's recent survey of art music after 1989 mentions Schnittke only three times: once as a performer of Pärt's *Tabula Rasa*, once in connection with "spiritual minimalism," and once alongside Bernd Alois Zimmermann as an ancestral "polystylist." Tellingly, Schnittke is cast as a composer already past, although the period 1989–1994 was the zenith of his prestige and popularity.[42] In her recent investigation of German musical identity, *Deutsche Musik*, musicologist Friederike Wißmann mentions Schnittke not at all, an oversight that seems particularly poignant for "the Russian with the German name" who took refuge near his life's end in Germany (and was applauded there) for reasons both personal and political.[43]

## VI

In an essay from 1973 called "Paradox as a Feature of Stravinsky's Musical Logic," Schnittke noted the disorientation caused by Igor Stravinsky's music. He called attention to the quotations and near-quotations in Stravinsky's Symphony in C, notably the opening bassoon melody in movement 4, which for Schnittke recalled the opening of Pyotr Tchaikovsky's Symphony no. 6, "Pathétique." Because of such references, Schnittke wrote, "We are shocked. We lose track of time, unsure of the hour, the day, the date. We even have doubts about the month and year."[44] As with Stravinsky, in Schnittke's hands, time becomes a flexible yet deceptive tool. "We feel the density of time itself," Slavoj Žižek says of Tarkovsky's films. "Things we see are markers of time."[45] Schnittke's markers—the glimpses of practices past and present—provide guidance for listeners. But they can also mislead; their outward familiarity gives false support.

In her poem "My God, It's Full of Stars," African-American poet Tracey K. Smith writes: "The frenzy of being. / I want it to be one notch below bedlam, like a radio without a dial. / Wide open, so everything floods in at once. / And sealed tight, so nothing escapes. Not even time, / Which should curl in on itself and look around like smoke. / So that I might be sitting now beside my father / As he raises a lit match to the bowl of his pipe / For the first time in the winter of 1959."[46] The title refers to the iconic line from Stanley Kubrick's film *2001*, when the protagonist, Dave Bowman, finally glimpses inside, and passes through, the mysterious alien monolith, hurtling through time and space. In the film's next scenes, time warps Bowman as we see him rapidly age. More than that, we see him seeing himself age.

Although written at a significant remove in time and space from Schnittke, Smith's poem conveys essential aspects of his Concerto Grosso no. 1: the frenzy of being, like a broken radio receiver, the frenzy of being which is the frenzy of time, untethered, swirling in Brownian motion, moving both forward and backward, enmeshing past and present. These essences explain the trilateral focus of a composition split between past, present, and future—tango, chorale, baroque, modern, postmodern, and beyond—the curls, gaps, and recollections, major and minor, across and within the composition. Two soloists blur into one, jockeying for position and sharing sonic embraces. What is past and what is present? Schnittke asks. What is memory and what is forgetting? What is chaos and what is order?

In the early 1990s, Savenko amplified the stakes in Schnittke's stylistic collisions:

> In general, the apocalypse is the most important theme of Schnittke's art. One can interpret it as the concrete character of the Last Judgment as in the . . . History of Doctor Johann Faust; it may be expressed as a metaphor for the death of culture as in the playful Concerto Grosso no. 1; or it may be heard as a form of individual psychological catastrophe, as in almost all of his instrumental concertos. Schnittke's beloved method of polystylism is itself apocalyptic, based as it is on colliding prepared blocks of cultural history in sudden contrasts in which their own time already no longer exists and the only possibility is a momentary reckoning before the face of death.[47]

She paints a bleak picture: Schnittke's polystylism strikes blocks of the past against one another, trying to spark temporary illumination, a catharsis before dying. As in Plato's cave, burdened by shadows, listeners catch glances of higher, illuminated truths.

Despairing interpretations of Schnittke's Concerto Grosso no. 1 predominated in the Soviet Union at its end and just after, overshadowing any possible redemption the composition might have conveyed. Composer Ivan Sokolov wrote in his 1992 history of twentieth-century composition: "The plot of the Concerto Grosso no. 1 may be interpreted as the tragic corrosion of culture. All the musical themes here traverse their own paths of destruction—from being structured to being taken apart, from the first impressions of loftiness to banality or impersonality." He concluded: "The device of decline is used repeatedly on different levels of the form."[48] This decline understandably conveyed grief. Krysa agreed with Nikitina about the Postludio and the work in general: "Schnittke's music always had that kind of sadness (*pechal'*)."[49]

We end on eggshells: the ghostly echo of the Toccata over the booming bass C. The final gesture is only just—the violins scraping strings behind the bridge. There is no conclusion. The C in the bass is an illusion of stability, as the Toccata reminiscence now seems. This is not the grace suggested as Monkey pushes the glasses across the table with her mind at *Stalker*'s end. But perhaps there is some reprieve. The violins' rising and falling gasps form the BACH motive. Or is any salvation doomed to waste away, like the Toccata fragment only "a momentary reckoning before the face of death"?

# APPENDIX

## COMMERCIAL RECORDINGS OF ALFRED SCHNITTKE, CONCERTO GROSSO NO. 1

Gidon Kremer and Tatiana Grindenko (violins), Gennady Rozhdestvensky (conductor), London Symphony Orchestra, recorded August 12-13, 1977 (Salzburg), LP Eurodisc/Melodia, Quadro SQ 25099 MK [n.d., 1977-78?]. Released on LP in USSR by Melodiia, S 10-13135 6, n.d. [1979?].

Oleh Krysa and Liana Isakadze (violins), Alfred Schnittke (prepared piano), Natalya Mandenova (harpsichord), Saulius Sondeckis (conductor), Georgian Chamber Orchestra, recorded September 3, 1983, Melodiia LP, S 10-21225-0004 (1984).

Christian Bergqvist and Patrik Swedrup (violins), Roland Pöntinen (harpsichord and prepared piano), Lev Markiz (conductor), New Stockholm Chamber Orchestra, recorded August 20–22, 1987, BIS CD, 377 (1987).

Gidon Kremer and Tatiana Grindenko (violins), Yuri Bashmet (conductor), Ensemble-Soloists, recorded May 1988, International Music Festival Leningrad, released on

A. Schnittke, *Concerto Grosso no. 1*, Gramzapis' CD, GCD 00067 (1988–90); and V. Martynov and A. Schnittke, *Come In/Concerto Grosso no. 1*, Melodiia LP, A10-00625-004 (1990); rereleased on *Schnittke: Orchestral Works & Chamber Music*, Col Legno CD, WWE 1CD 20510 (2000); and *Schnittke: Concerto Grosso Nos. 1 & 2*, Alto CD, ALC 1341 (2017).

Gidon Kremer and Tatiana Grindenko (violins), Yuri Smirnov (harpsichord and prepared piano), Heinrich Schiff (conductor), Chamber Orchestra of Europe, Deutsche Grammophon CD 429 413-2 (1990); rereleased on *Music from Eastern Europe: Schnittke, Lutosławski, Ligeti*, Deutsche Grammophon CD, 439 452-2 (1994).

Eleonora Turovsky and Natalya Turovsky (violins), Catherine Perrin (harpsichord and prepared piano), Yuli Turovsky (conductor), Musici de Montréal, Chandos CD, CHAN 9590 (1997).

Marco Serino and Ludovico Tramma (violins), Flavio Emilio Scogna (conductor), Ensemble "Il Terzo Suono," Dynamic CD, S 2030 (1999).

Victor Kuleshov and Ilya Ioff (violins), Julia Lev (harpsichord and piano), Arcady Shteinlukht (conductor), St. Petersburg Mozarteum Chamber Orchestra, Manchester Files CD, CDMAN 175 (2004).

ARRANGEMENT FOR FLUTE AND OBOE (1986)

Alfred Schnittke, *Concerto Grosso no. 1; Symphony no. 9*, Sharon Bezaly (flute), Christopher Cowie (oboe), Owain Arwel Hughes (conductor), Cape Philharmonic Orchestra, BIS CD, 1727 (2009).

*Bach/Schnittke*, with J. S. Bach, Concerto for 2 violins and strings, and Alfred Schnittke, *Moz-Art à la Haydn* for 2 violins and strings, Maria Alikhanova (flute), Dmitri Bulgakov (oboe), Misha Rachlevsky (conductor), Chamber Orchestra Kremlin, Quartz Music CD, QTZ 2083 (2010).

# ADDITIONAL SOURCES
## FOR READING AND
## LISTENING

As this book's appendix shows, there is an abundance of recordings of Alfred Schnittke's Concerto Grosso no. 1. Any of the Gidon Kremer and Tatiana Grindenko recordings or the Oleh Krysa and Liana Isakadze recording will provide a good starting point. Kremer and Grindenko's recently reissued live recording from 1988 is raw and energetic. Krysa and Isakadze's recording, particularly its Tango, is powerful yet restrained; a unique document, it features the composer himself at the prepared piano, performing with more grace and more bombast than most. The recent Bomba St. Petersburg recording also stands out for its interpretative risk-taking, as does the 2009 live recording by the Boston ensemble A Far Cry, one of the most thoughtful, persuasive presentations available (https://vimeo.com/14901472).

The best sources for information about Schnittke's life and works are spread across three languages: Russian, German, and English. Unfortunately, a majority of the literature remains in the first two of these, although English is slowly catching up. There is no up-to-date, reliable, scholarly biography of Schnittke in any language. *A Schnittke Reader*, edited by Alexander Ivashkin (Bloomington and Indianapolis: Indiana University Press, 2002), provides a good alternative point of entry. Nonetheless, the interviews with the composer in this volume should be read for what they are: reminiscences by a composer in his mid-fifties still recovering from a serious stroke. Gavin Dixon's recent *Schnittke Studies* (London and New York: Routledge, 2017) gives a representative sampling of recent scholarship on the composer.

For details of Schnittke's early work (through his Symphony no. 1), see my *Such Freedom, If Only Musical: Unofficial Soviet Music during the Thaw* (New York: Oxford University Press, 2009), as well as my "Selling Schnittke," in *The Oxford Handbook of Musical Censorship*, ed. Patricia Hall (Oxford: Oxford University Press, 2017). My entry for Schnittke in Oxford Bibliographies Online contains annotated citations of other standard sources. Richard Taruskin's *The Oxford History of Western Music*, Vol. 5: *The Late Twentieth Century* (Oxford: Oxford University Press, 2005), especially chapter 68, "After Everything," provides a broader sociocultural and political context for Schnittke's output.

I treat many of the topics discussed here at greater length in my book manuscript, *Sonic Overload: Polystylism as Cultural Practice in the Late USSR*, which covers Schnittke's music from his Symphony no. 1 through the end of his career, alongside the music of Ukrainian composer Valentin Silvestrov from the same period.

# NOTES

## CHAPTER 1

1 See Peter Cossé, liner notes to Gidon Kremer and Tatiana Grindenko, *Sibelius Violin Concerto/Schnittke Concerto Grosso*, Eurodisc/Melodia LP, Quadro SQ 25099 MK (n.d. [1977–78?]); Universal, ix; *Critical Edition*, 12.

2 Sara Miller, "Listening to Jack White [The Mail]," *New Yorker*, April 3, 2017, 5.

3 Klaus Geitel, "Uraufführungen von Schnittke und Rihm . . .," *Das Orchester* 32 (1984): 1090. Unless otherwise indicated, all translations are mine.

4 Quoted in M. Babak, dir., *Ia, nemetskii kompozitor iz Rossii . . . Monolog Al'freda Shnitke* [film] (Tsentral'naia Studiia Dokumental'nykh fil'mov, Soveksportfil'm, and Feliksverlag, 1990), 00:11–00:56; also *Reader*, 21.

5 Karl Schlögel, *Moscow*, trans. Helen Atkins (London: Reaktion, 2005; 1st ed. 1984), 207.

6 Peter J. Schmelz, "Alfred Schnittke's *Nagasaki*: Soviet Nuclear Culture, Radio Moscow, and the Global Cold War," *Journal of the American Musicological Society* 62, no. 2 (2009): 413–74.

7 See Peter J. Schmelz, *Such Freedom, If Only Musical: Unofficial Soviet Music during the Thaw* (New York: Oxford University Press, 2009), 235–41.

8 Compare liner notes to Alfred Schnittke, *Violin Concertos no. 3 and no. 4*, BIS CD 517 (1991), 4; and *Gody*, 84.

9 See Schmelz, *Such Freedom, If Only Musical*; also *Gody*, 53–54.

10 Al'fred Shnitke and Elena Petrushanskaia, "Iz besed o rabote v kino," *Muzykal'naia akademiia*, no. 2 (1999): 93–94; and K. E. Razlogov and V. Iu. Khrapachev, "Muzyka v zvukozritel'nom sinteze (Teoriia i praktiki: interv'iu s kompozitorami E. Artem'evym, G. Kancheli, I. Shvartsem i A. Shnitke)," *Voprosy filosofii*, no. 2 (1988): 137–39.

11 See Laura Pontieri, *Soviet Animation and the Thaw of the 1960s: Not Only for Children* (New Barnet, UK, and Bloomington: John Libbey and Indiana University Press, 2012).

12 Al'fred Shnitke and Ol'ga Martynenko, "Al'fred Shnitke: Istina—v mnogoobrazii," *Moskovskie novosti*, May 14, 1989, 16.

13 *Reader*, 90.

14 Hannelore Gerlach, ed., *Fünfzig sowjetische Komponisten der Gegenwart* (Leipzig and Dresden: Peters, 1984), 363–64.

15 See Juilliard Manuscript Collection, SCHN_COLL_521, "Variant for the improvised cadenza to the II movement (for any kind of rock-group)" (*Variant improvizatsionnoi kadentsii ko II chasti [dlia rok-gruppy liubogo sostava]*).

16 Alfred Schnittke, "The Third Movement of Berio's *Sinfonia*: Stylistic Counterpoint, Thematic and Formal Unity in Context of Polystylistics, Broadening the Concept of Thematicism (1970s)," in *Reader*, 216–24; also *Stat'i*, 88–91.

17 "Obsuzhdaem Simfoniiu A. Shnitke," *Sovetskaia muzyka*, no. 10 (1974): 19.

18 Ibid.

19 Yurii Kholopov, "Nashi v Anglii: II. Elena Firsova," in *Muzyka iz byvshego SSSR*, vol. 2, ed. Valeriia Tsenova (Moscow: Kompozitor, 1996), 284–85.

20 *Gody*, 75.

21 Peter J. Schmelz, "What Was 'Shostakovich,' and What Came Next?," *Journal of Musicology* 24, no. 3 (2007): 319–22.

22 *Gody*, 76.

23 Aleksandr Zhurbin, *Orfei, Evridika i ia* (Moscow: Eksmo, 2006), 281.

24 *Gody*, 69–72.

25 Ibid., 71; and Shnitke and Petrushanskaia, "Iz besed o rabote v kino," 93.

26 *Gody*, 75.

27 Ludwig van Beethoven, *Violin Concerto in D*, Gidon Kremer, Academy of St. Martin in the Fields, Philips CD, 410 549–2 (1982). The recording was made in 1980. Although all the cadenzas on the recording are credited to Schnittke, Kremer omits several measures in the first-movement cadenza (mm. 91–98), does not use Schnittke's published cadenza for the second movement at all, and alters the published first version of the third-movement cadenza (there are two variants of the last cadenza). On the recording, the final cadenza includes an opening section not found in the score, consisting of several flourishes based on the movement's main and subsidiary themes; it also omits several measures (e.g., mm. 5–10, 14–15) and alters others (e.g., mm. 18–21). Kremer and the ensemble perform the remainder of the third-movement cadenza as written. See Alfred Schnittke, *Kadenzen zum Konzert für Violine und Orchester von Ludwig van Beethoven* (Hamburg: Sikorski, 2015). See also Gidon Kremer, *In@rodnyi artist* (Moscow: Novoe Literaturnoe Obozrenie, 2006), 488–92. This, the Russian

version of his two German autobiographies, is updated and corrected and at times diverges from the German (e.g., 707–10). I nonetheless refer to the German versions to aid readers unfamiliar with Russian: Gidon Kremer, *Obertöne* (Salzburg and Vienna: Residenz, 1997); and Gidon Kremer, *Zwischen Welten* (Munich and Zurich: Piper, 2003).

28  Allan Kozinn, "Fresh Insights into Standard Works," *New York Times*, March 13, 1983, H32. See also Peter J. Schmelz, "Selling Schnittke: Late Soviet Censorship in the Cold War Marketplace," in *The Oxford Handbook of Musical Censorship*, ed. Patricia Hall (Oxford: Oxford University Press, 2017), 433–35.

29  Bryan Crimp, "Gidon Kremer," *Gramophone*, October 1981, 36; and Wolf-Eberhard von Lewinski, *Gidon Kremer: Interviews—Tatsachen—Meinungen* (Mainz: Goldmann Schott, 1982), 100–103. Schnittke composed a number of other cadenzas for canonic concertos, primarily for works by W. A. Mozart, including his piano concertos K. 491, no. 24, in C minor (1975); K. 467, no. 21, in C major (1980); K. 503, no. 25, in C major (1983); and K. 39, no. 2, in B-flat major (1990); as well as for Mozart's Bassoon Concerto, K. 191 (1983). None is as conceptually—or compositionally—dense as the Beethoven Violin Concerto cadenzas.

30  *Gody*, 79. A draft listing numerous other possible names for the composition is reproduced in *Besedy*, 246–47 (1994).

31  David Fanning, liner notes to *Kremer Plays Schnittke*, Deutsche Grammophon CD, 445 520–2 (1990), 4.

32  For more on humor in Schnittke, see E. Chigareva in *Posviashchaetsia* 7 (2010): 127; also in her *Khudozhestvennyi mir Al'freda Shnitke* (Saint Petersburg: Kompozitor, 2012), 146–64.

33  *Besedy*, 246–47 (1994).

34  Gottfried Kraus (trans. E. D. Echols), liner notes to Gidon Kremer and Tatjana Grindenko, *Ausgewählte Duos von Mozart, Haydn, Reger, Bartók, Schnittke*, Eurodisc/Melodia LP, 200083-405 (1977).

35  Svetlana Savenko, "Portret khudozhnika v zrelosti," *Sovetskaia muzyka*, no. 9 (1981): 38.

36  Kholopova, 119.

37  *Reader*, 45; and Al'fred Shnitke and Arkadii Petrov, "Concerto Grosso no. 1 (1975)," in *Posviashchaetsia* 3 (2003): 49. The printed date for this interview must be an error; the correct year is probably 1977.

38  Ibid.

39  Kholopova, 119.

40  Oleh Krysa, interview with author, Rochester, NY, April 20, 2017.

41  The quotations in this and the preceding sentence are from Universal, ix.

42  Krysa, interview.

43  Alfred Schnittke, "Ligeti's Orchestral Micropolyphony (1970s)," in *Reader*, 225; also *Stat'i*, 66.

44 At rehearsal 1 there are divergences between recordings. In Kremer and Grindenko's versions on Eurodisc/Melodia and later Deutsche Grammophon, as well as in Lev Markiz's recording on BIS, the harpsichord plays isolated pitches underneath the soloists, a harbinger of the figuration in measures 30–31 in the score. Krysa and Isakadze's recording does not include this. The figuration occurs in no published version of the score, but it does appear in a copy of the autograph score (first version) at Goldsmiths, University of London, previously owned by conductor Saulius Sondeckis. Yet in the revised score of the work at Goldsmiths in measures 18–21, the harpsichord's lower staff is scribbled out, presumably excising notes it once had. The editors of the critical edition omit this harpsichord part because Schnittke does not perform it in Krysa and Isakadze's recording. See *Critical Edition*, 95.

45 Kenneth Gloag, *Postmodernism in Music* (Cambridge: Cambridge University Press, 2012), 133.

46 Ibid., 136.

47 For a good introduction, see Sergey Kuznetsov, "Postmodernism in Russia," in *International Postmodernism: Theory and Literary Practice*, ed. Hans Bertens and Douwe Fokkema (Amsterdam and Philadelphia: John Benjamins, 1997), 451–60 (esp. the bibliography); and Mikhail N. Epstein, Alexander A. Genis, and Slobodanka M. Vladiv-Glover, *Russian Postmodernism: New Perspectives on Post-Soviet Culture* (New York and Oxford: Berghahn Books, 1999). See also Zh. Kozina, "Muzykal'nyi postmodernizm—khimera ili real'nost'?," *Sovetskaia muzyka*, no. 9 (1989): 117–19 (an overview of the December 1988 number of *Neue Zeitschrift für Musik* that addressed musical postmodernism); and E. Iu. Andreeva, *Postmodernizm: Iskusstvo vtoroi poloviny XX–nachala XXI veka* (Saint Petersburg: Azbuka-Klassika, 2007).

48 Svetlana Savenko, "V rakurse postmoderna," in *Istoriia otechestvennoi muzyki vtoroi poloviny XX veka*, ed. T. N. Levaia (Saint Petersburg: Kompozitor, 2005), 547.

49 Alexander Ivashkin, "Who's Afraid of Socialist Realism?," *Slavonic and East European Review* 92, no. 3 (2014): 442.

50 Savenko, "V rakurse postmoderna," 547; and Savenko, "Portret khudozhnika v zrelosti," 38.

51 The classic English-language introduction is Malcolm Hamrick Brown, "The Soviet Russian Concepts of 'Intonazia' and 'Musical Imagery,'" *Musical Quarterly* 60, no. 4 (1974): 557–67.

52 Savenko, "V rakurse postmoderna," 547.

53 Compare Savenko, "V rakurse postmoderna," 547 n. 9; and Ivashkin, "Who's Afraid of Socialist Realism?," 442.

54 The standard treatment of Berio's *Sinfonia* remains David Osmond-Smith, *Playing on Words: A Guide to Luciano Berio's Sinfonia* (London: Royal Musical Association, 1985).

55  For an example of such an approach, see François Cusset, *French Theory: How Foucault, Derrida, Deleuze, & Co. Transformed the Intellectual Life of the United States*, trans. Jeff Fort with Josephine Berganza and Marlon Jones (Minneapolis: University of Minnesota Press, 2008).

56  See Peter J. Schmelz, *Sonic Overload: Polystylism as Cultural Practice in the Late USSR*.

57  Savenko, "Portret khudozhnika v zrelosti," 38.

58  Jörg Polzin, quoted in program booklet for *Komponistenportrait Alfred Schnittke*, September 17 and 18, 1988, 38th Berliner Festwochen 88, 22.

59  Elena Dvoskina, "Tat'iana Grindenko: Novyi put'," *Muzykal'naia akademiia*, no. 2 (2003): 50. See J. Peter Burkholder and Claude V. Palisca, *Norton Anthology of Western Music*, Vol. 3: *The Twentieth Century and After*, 7th ed. (New York: W. W. Norton, 2014), 861–93; and Richard Taruskin, *The Oxford History of Western Music*, Vol. 5: *The Late Twentieth Century* (Oxford: Oxford University Press, 2005), 463–71.

## CHAPTER 2

1  See John Caldwell, "Toccata," *Grove Music Online, Oxford Music Online*, http://www.oxfordmusiconline.com/subscriber/article/grove/music/28035.

2  Valentina Kholopova and Evgeniia Chigareva, *Al'fred Shnitke: Ocherk zhizni i tvorchestva* (Moscow: Sovetskii kompozitor, 1990), 74.

3  *Festschrift*, 87.

4  See Lisa Jakelski, *Making New Music in Cold War Poland: The Warsaw Autumn Festival, 1956–1968* (Oakland: University of California Press, 2017), 177. A slightly earlier Polish example is Andrzej Koszewski's *Concerto grosso all'antica* (1947; published in 1984).

5  Shnitke and Petrov, "Concerto Grosso no. 1," 48.

6  *Gody*, 60–61. I discuss this phenomenon in greater detail in Schmelz, *Sonic Overload*.

7  *Gody*, 37.

8  The genesis of the German program note warrants discussion. The most-cited source for it is the 1994 Sikorksi Festschrift for Schnittke (p. 100), but the first publication of the German program note that I am aware of appeared in the program booklet accompanying the premiere of choreographer John Neumeier's ballet *Othello* from late January 1985, meaning the note must date at the very latest from the beginning of 1985 (see chapter 5 in this book). The "note" here is credited to an interview Schnittke gave to Jörg Polzin. It was also quoted in Gottfried Blumenstein, "Die Kunst der Verschmelzung," *Wochenpost*, no. 10 (1989): 15. The 1985 and 1994 versions of the "note" differ in several respects: light revisions occur throughout, and the text has been

rearranged. The text in the Festschrift is credited only to Schnittke. The Russian program note first appeared only in *Besedy*, 243–44 (1994), where Ivashkin dates it to the "late 1970s" (konets 1970-kh g.). Schnittke probably wrote it just after he completed his Concerto Grosso no. 1, in 1977 or 1978. Savenko cites ideas resembling those in the German note in her 1981 "Portret khudozhnika v zrelosti"; her reported source is a program note by Schnittke for the Eurodisc record company. Yet Peter Cossé contributed the note to the European release of this recording by Kremer and Grindenko; the note on the Melodiya release was by Savenko herself. Savenko's liner notes also seem to paraphrase certain of Schnittke's remarks from the German program note. There thus appears to be another, earlier, unpublished variant of Schnittke's German comments, or perhaps Schnittke was voicing these ideas, particularly those about banality, for some time—including to Savenko—before he told them to Polzin. See Savenko, "Portret khudozhnika v zrelosti," 38–39 (esp. 39 n. 9); Savenko, liner notes to Melodiia LP, 33 S 10-13135-6 (see appendix); and Shnitke and Petrov, "Concerto Grosso no. 1," 48.

9  Gerlach, *Fünfzig sowjetische Komponisten der Gegenwart*, 366. Gerlach indicates that the source of Schnittke's comments is an interview with her from "2.7.1977 Berlin."

10  *Reader*, 45–46; original Russian in *Stat'i*, 103–4.

11  Ibid.

12  Ibid. (translation amended).

13  Festschrift, 100.

14  Ibid. This is the statement Savenko paraphrased in her Melodiya LP program notes.

15  Ibid.

16  Ibid.

17  Shnitke and Petrov, "Concerto Grosso no. 1," 48.

18  Ibid.

19  Al'fred Shnitke and Arkadii Petrov, "Pervaia simfoniia: Besedy pered prem'eroi (7–8.II.74)," in *Posviashchaetsia* 3 (2003): 44.

20  Other writers describe varying numbers of stylistic components to the work. See Savenko, "Portret khudozhnika v zrelosti," 38; and Ivan Sokolov, *Muzykal'naia kompozitsiia XX veka: Dialektika tvorchestva* (Moscow: Muzyka, 1992), 65.

21  Ivana Medić, "The Sketches for Alfred Schnittke's Symphony no. 3 and What They (Don't) Tell Us," *Muzikologija/Musicology*, no. 15 (2013): 169–213, http://www.doiserbia.nb.rs/img/doi/1450-9814/2013/1450-98141315169M.pdf; as well as Ivana Medić, "'Crucifixus etiam pro nobis': Representations of the Cross in Alfred Schnittke's Symphony no. 2, 'St. Florian,'" in *Schnittke Studies*, ed. Gavin Dixon (London and New York: Routledge, 2017), 3–29.

22 Jean-Benoît Tremblay, "Polystylism and Narrative Potential in the Music of Alfred Schnittke" (Ph.D. diss., University of British Columbia, 2007), 140; and Victoria Adamenko, *Neo-mythologism in Music from Scriabin and Schoenberg to Schnittke and Crumb* (Hillsdale, NY: Pendragon Press, 2007), 247–48.

23 SCG. The sketches are divided into two sets: A3 includes twenty-six sheets; A4 has fifteen.

24 See Peter Wortsman, "Introduction: The Displaced Person's Guide to Nowhere," in Adelbert von Chamisso, *Peter Schlemiel: The Man Who Sold His Shadow*, trans. Peter Wortsman (New York: Fromm International, 1993), xiii.

25 The citations in this paragraph are to A4:10 and A4:3, SCG.

26 These initials appear at the bottom of A4:12: Gidon Kremer, G–D–E–E; and Tatjana Grindenko, A–A–A–G–D–E (repeated once in its entirety with the G and E displaced down and up an octave, respectively).

27 Schnittke to Valentin Silvestrov, letter postmarked January 14, 1978, Paul Sacher Stiftung, Sammlung Valentin Silvestrov, Correspondence.

28 Kholopova, 119.

29 *Reader*, 45; and *Stat'i*, 103.

30 Shnitke and Petrov, "Concerto Grosso no. 1," 49.

31 For more on *Glass Harmonica* as "political criticism," see Pontieri, *Soviet Animation and the Thaw of the 1960s*, 147–67.

32 Tremblay, "Polystylism and Narrative Potential," 157.

33 Aleksandr Mitta quoted in *Sovetskii fil'm*, no. 1 (1976): 29; cited in E. Gromov, "Zhanr i tvorcheskoe mnogoobrazie sovetskogo kinoiskusstva," in *Zhanry kino*, ed. V. I. Fomin (Moscow: Iskusstvo, 1979), 13–30, at 28. See also Mitta's essay in the same volume: "Orientir—logika zhanra," 309–18.

34 Shnitke and Petrov, "Concerto Grosso no. 1," 49.

35 Ibid. See also Tamara Burde, *Zum Leben und Schaffen des Komponisten Alfred Schnittke* (Kludenbach: Gehann-Musik-Verlag, 1993), 52; and Kholopova, 119.

36 Michael Baumgartner, "Partisanenparabel/Passionsmusik: Alfred Schnittkes Filmmusik zu Larissa Schepitkos *Die Erhöhung*," in *Alfred Schnittke: Analyse—Interpretation—Rezeption*, ed. Amrei Flechsig and Christian Storch (Hildesheim: Georg Olms Verlag, 2010), 198. See also *Alfred Schnittke: Film Music Edition*, Frank Strobel, Rundfunk-Sinfonieorchester Berlin, Capriccio CD, C7196 (2015).

37 Tremblay, "Polystylism and Narrative Potential," 161–64.

38 Ibid., 150.

39 Shnitke and Petrov, "Concerto Grosso no. 1," 49.

40 Kholopova, 119.

41 Sokolov delves deeper into the twelve-tone construction of the succeeding section in his *Muzykal'naia kompozitsiia XX veka*, 66–71. For further background, see Peter J. Schmelz, "Shostakovich's 'Twelve-Tone' Compositions

and the Politics and Practice of Soviet Serialism," in *Shostakovich and His World*, ed. Laurel E. Fay (Princeton: Princeton University Press, 2004), 303–54.

42 Burkholder and Palisca, *Norton Anthology of Western Music*, 3: 893.

## CHAPTER 3

1 See Dale E. Monson et al., "Recitative," *Grove Music Online, Oxford Music Online*, http://www.oxfordmusiconline.com/subscriber/article/grove/music/23019.

2 Kholopova, 119; and Don Anderson, program notes to Toronto Symphony Orchestra concerts featuring Concerto Grosso no. 1 on May 26 and 27, 2004, *Performance*, March/May 2004, 6.

3 Harvey Sachs, liner notes to *Music from Eastern Europe*, Deutsche Grammophon CD, 439 452–2 (1994), 7; and Richard Tiedman, review of various Schnittke recordings, *Tempo*, no. 182 (1992): 48.

4 Krysa, interview.

5 Tremblay first identified a Berg quotation at this moment but did not specify its exact source in the Violin Concerto or the BACH reference just before it. Tremblay, "Polystylism and Narrative Potential," 132.

6 Kholopova and Chigareva, *Al'fred Shnitke*, 126.

7 Tremblay, "Polystylism and Narrative Potential," 132.

8 The quotations also resemble the use of Beethoven's Symphony no. 5, movement 4, at the climax of the first movement of Schnittke's Symphony no. 1 and the appearance of a citation from the first movement of the same Beethoven symphony at the very end of the Overture to Schnittke's *Gogol Suite* (1976). Although given the conductor's central role in orchestrating and arranging the suite, credit for this last reference might belong as much to Gennady Rozhdestvensky as to Schnittke.

9 *Gody*, 48. See also Shnitke and Petrushanskaia, "Iz besed o rabote v kino," 96; and Schmelz, *Sonic Overload*.

10 Schnittke, "Ligeti's Orchestral Micropolyphony," 225.

11 Ibid.

12 Ibid., 228.

13 See Tremblay on the rhythmic calculations in the score, in "Polystylism and Narrative Potential," 148-49.

14 Wortsman, "Introduction," xiv; and Adelbert von Chamisso, "Peter Schlemiel," in *Tales of the German Imagination from the Brothers Grimm to Ingeborg Bachmann*, ed. Peter Wortsman (London: Penguin, 2012), 116.

15 Chamisso, "Peter Schlemiel," 102.

16 Ibid., 130, 95.

17  Ibid., 142, 143.

18  Ibid., 117.

## CHAPTER 4

1  Chigareva, *Khudozhestvennyi mir Al'freda Shnitke*, 149.

2  Ibid.

3  See S. Sondetskis, "Nezabyvaemoe," in *Posviashchaetsia* 5 (2006): 11; reprinted (in slightly condensed form) in *Al'fred Shnitke: Stat'i, interv'iu. Vospominaniia o kompozitore*, ed. Andrei Khrzhanovskii (Moscow: Arcadia/Izdatel' M. A. Troianker, 2014), 171–76.

4  *Reader*, 45; and *Stat'i*, 103.

5  Donal Henahan, "Violinist: Gidon Kremer Plays in a Different Way," *New York Times*, March 27, 1979, C12; and Eleanor Blau, "Soviet Puzzle: 'Greatest Violinist in the World,'" *New York Times*, August 27, 1980, C20.

6  *Gody*, 24.

7  Ibid., 82.

8  "Five Minutes with . . . Sofia Gubaidulina," *Strings* 26, no. 3 (2011): 20.

9  Liner notes to Melodiia LP, S 10-13135-6, n.d. [1979?].

10  Joachim Kaiser, "Zarte, aufregende Abenteuer: Gidon Kremer, Tatjana Grindenko und das Wilnaer Kammerorchester," *Süddeutsche Zeitung*, November 21, 1977, 14.

11  See Dvoskina, "Tat'iana Grindenko: Novyi put'," 50; and Peter J. Schmelz, "From Scriabin to Pink Floyd: The ANS Synthesizer and the Politics of Soviet Music between Thaw and Stagnation," in *Sound Commitments: Avant-Garde Music and the Sixties*, ed. Robert Adlington (New York: Oxford University Press, 2009), 267–68.

12  Dvoskina, "Tat'iana Grindenko: Novyi put'," 50.

13  Shnitke and Petrov, "Concerto Grosso no. 1," 50.

14  *Critical Edition*, 7–9.

15  Schnittke gives Kremer's birthdate as February 26, but in standard references (Oxford Music Online; *Die Musik in Geschichte und Gegenwart* [MGG Online]), it is listed as February 27.

16  *Besedy*, 265 (2005).

17  Sondetskis, "Nezabyvaemoe," 12.

18  From Alexander Ivashkin, "Preface," and Aleksei Vul'fson and Elena Isaenko, "Editorial Notes," both in *Critical Edition*, 7, 9–10.

19  See Schmelz, "Selling Schnittke," 423–27 and passim.

20  All from Sondetskis, "Nezabyvaemoe," 12.

21  Ibid., 13.

22  Ibid., 14.

23  Dvoskina, "Tat'iana Grindenko: Novyi put'," 50.

24  Krysa, interview.

25  *Reader,* 232.

26  Sondetskis, "Nezabyvaemoe," 16.

27  Ibid., 16–17.

28  Ibid., 15–17; Kremer, *In@rodnyi artist,* 512; and Kremer, *Zwischen Welten,* 239.

29  Sondetskis, "Nezabyvaemoe," 17.

30  Kremer, *In@rodnyi artist,* 512; and Kremer, *Zwischen Welten,* 239.

31  A. G. Shnitke and V. M. Sheternikov, in Liudmila Stepchkova, *Perelistyvaia stranitsy pamiati* (Moscow: n.p., 2002), 99; quoted in *Posviashchaetsia* 8 (2011): 164.

32  Sondetskis, "Nezabyvaemoe," 18.

33  These dates are based on programs held at the Estonian Theatre and Music Museum, Tallinn. My thanks to Kevin Karnes for sharing this information.

34  Sondetskis, "Nezabyvaemoe," 15, 18. Sondeckis's calculations for the number of performances on the tour featuring Schnittke's and Pärt's music are inconsistent. At least one of the figures he provides must be incorrect (i.e., off by one).

35  Lewinski, *Gidon Kremer,* 111–12.

36  Kremer, *In@rodnyi artist,* 515; and Kremer, *Zwischen Welten,* 243.

37  *Reader,* 232.

38  Kremer, *In@rodnyi artist,* 515; and Kremer, *Zwischen Welten,* 241.

39  Alexander Ivashkin, *Alfred Schnittke* (London: Phaidon, 1996), 146–49.

40  *Reader,* 233.

41  The German and Russian versions of this statement diverge. Compare Kremer, *In@rodnyi artist,* 515; and Kremer, *Zwischen Welten,* 243.

42  Cossé, liner notes.

43  The two Leopold Mozart duets were the last of the six duets from his "Twelve Duets for two violins" performed by Kremer and Grindenko on the *Ausgewählte Duos* LP. See also Sondetskis, "Nezabyvaemoe," 15, 18.

44  In Achim Hofer, ed., *"Sei mir nicht böse für mein langes Schweigen": Der Briefwechsel zwischen Alfred Schnittke und Tilo Medek (1968–1989)* (Mainz: Schott, 2010), 117.

45  Krysa, interview.

46  Melodiia LP, 33 S 10-10831-2. See http://lianaisakadze.com/ru/2011-03-10-12-12-07, for a fuller discography (absent catalog numbers and release dates; accessed December 22, 2018). Note especially her fine rendering of Schnittke's Violin Sonata no. 2 and Maurice Ravel's Violin Sonata on a 1978 Melodiia LP (33 S 10-10831-2).

47  Ulrich Schreiber, "Metamusik [Review of Alfred Schnittke: *Concerto Grosso I; Konzert für Oboe, Harfe und Streichorchester; Konzert für Klavier und Streichorchester,* BIS CD-377]," *Neue Musikzeitung* 37 (June–July 1988): 34.

48  Kholopova and Chigareva, *Al'fred Shnitke,* 127.

## CHAPTER 5

1 The rehearsal and measure numbers in the Universal score and the *Critical Edition* diverge in movement 5, Rondo. I provide both sets of numbers for this movement, with the Universal score always preceding the *Critical Edition*.

2 *Reader*, 234.

3 See also Gordon Marsh, "Schnittke's Polystylistic Schemata: Textural Progression in the Concerti Grossi," in *Schnittke Studies*, ed. Gavin Dixon · (London and New York: Routledge, 2017), 115–20.

4 *Reader*, 234.

5 Chigareva, *Khudozhestvennyi mir Al'freda Shnitke*, 148; quoting *Posviashchaetsia* 3 (2003): 279.

6 *Besedy*, 142 (1994).

7 Kremer, *Obertöne*, 198.

8 Tat'iana Cherednichenko, *Muzykal'nyi zapas. Problemy. Portrety. Sluchai* (Moscow: Novoe Literaturnoe Obozrenie, 2002), 69.

9 Ibid.

10 Tremblay, "Polystylism and Narrative Potential," 159–60.

11 See, for example, Maria Kostakeva, *Im Strom der Zeiten und der Welten: Das Spätwerk von Alfred Schnittke* (Saarbrücken: Pfau-Verlag, 2005), 34; and Dorothea Redepenning, "Inszenierungen von 'Gut' und 'Böse' in Alfred Schnittkes Instrumentalmusik," in *Alfred Schnittke: Analyse—Interpretation—Rezeption*, ed. Amrei Flechsig and Christian Storch (Hildesheim: Georg Olms Verlag, 2010), 71–90. For a more detailed critique of this received wisdom, see Schmelz, *Sonic Overload*, chapter 3, "Schnittke and the Popular."

12 Savenko, "Portret khudozhnika v zrelosti," 38, 39.

13 Ibid. See also Liza Knapp, "Tsvetaeva's 'Blackest of Black' (*Naicherneishii*) Pushkin," in *Under the Sky of My Africa: Alexander Pushkin and Blackness*, ed. Catherine Nepomnyashchy, Nicole Svobodny, and Ludmilla A. Trigos (Evanston, IL: Northwestern University Press, 2006), 300–301 n. 29.

14 Savenko, "Portret khudozhnika v zrelosti," 39, 39 n. 9.

15 *Reader*, 235.

16 Thomas Mann, "Tonio Kröger," in *Death in Venice and Seven Other Stories*, trans. H. T. Lowe-Porter (New York: Vintage, 1989), 102.

17 Gerlach, *Fünfzig sowjetische Komponisten der Gegenwart*, 364.

18 *Reader*, 45.

19 From the January 16, 1980, meeting of the Komissiia (Sektsiia) simfonicheskoi i kamernoi muzyki Moskovskoi organizatsii Soiuza kompozitorov RSFSR, quoted in Kholopova and Chigareva, *Al'fred Shnitke*, 123 n. 26.

20 Everything in this paragraph is from Kholopova, 118–19.

21 Kremer, *Obertöne*, 198.

22 Chigareva, *Khudozhestvennyi mir Al'freda Shnitke,* 31.

23 Krysa, interview.

24 Walter-Wolfgang Sparrer, "Von den Gefahren des Teuflischen: Vermischte Bemerkungen zu Alfred Schnittke, seinen Opern und seinem letzten Stil," *MusikTexte* 61 (October 1995): 28–32, at 28.

25 Rudolf Klein, "Neues aus Wiener Konzertsälen," *Österreichische Musikzeitschrift* 33, no. 1 (1978): 45–46.

26 Kaiser, "Zarte, aufregende Abenteuer," 14.

27 Harald Wihler, "Magier mit der Geige: Das 'kleine' Konzert der russischen Gäste," *Bonner Rundschau,* November 29, 1977.

28 Letter dated February 25, 1978, in Valentin Sil'vestrov and Marina Nest'eva, *Muzyka—eto penie mira o samom sebe . . . Sokrovenny razgovory i vzgliady so storony: besedy, stat'i, pis'ma* (Kiev: n.p., 2004), 237–38.

29 Ibid., 237. Silvestrov uses the term *estrada* here, literally "variety stage."

30 Ibid., 238. See Peter Schmelz, "Valentin Silvestrov and the Echoes of Music History," *Journal of Musicology* 31, no. 2 (2014): 246, 248.

31 Sil'vestrov and Nest'eva, *Muzyka—eto penie mira o samom sebe,* 237–38.

32 Andrzej Chłopecki, Bogusław Kaczyński, and Olgierd Pisarenko, "Sznitke: Concerto grosso," *Ruch Muzyczny* 23, no. 24 (November 19, 1978): 9.

33 Ibid.

34 Ibid.

35 Boris Schwarz, "Continuum: Soviet Avant-Garde Music," *Musical America/ High Fidelity* 31 (June 1981): 29–30 (*Musical America*).

36 Boris Schwarz, "Continuum: All-Schnittke Program," *Musical America/High Fidelity* 32 (June 1982): 26–27 (*Musical America*). Schwarz does not mention the composition in his discussions of the events of 1977 or of Schnittke in *Music and Musical Life in Soviet Russia, Enlarged Edition: 1917–1981* (Bloomington: Indiana University Press, 1983), 598–606, 631–34.

37 N. Dimitriadi, liner notes to Melodiia LP, S 10-21225-0004.

38 See Savenko, "Portret khudozhnika v zrelosti," 40.

39 Kholopova and Chigareva, *Al'fred Shnitke,* 128.

40 T. Levaia, "Sovetskaia muzyka: Dialog desiatiletii," in *Sovetskaia muzyka 70-80-kh godov: Stil' i stilevye dialogi,* ed. V. B. Val'kova (Moscow: GMNI im. Gnesinykh, 1985–86), 11.

41 M. E. Tarakanov, *Sovetskaia muzyka vchera i segodnia (Novyi vzgliad na istoriiu i problem segodniashego dnia), Iskusstvo* 5 (Moscow: Znanie, 1989), 49–50, 36. See also Tarakanov's discussion of Schnittke's Concerto Grosso no. 1 in his *Simfoniia i instrumental'nyi kontsert v russkoi-sovetskoi muzyke (60-70-e gody). Puti razvitiia* (Moscow: Sovetskii kompozitor, 1988), 177–85.

42 L. D. Nikitina, *Sovetskaia muzyka: istoriia i sovremennost'* (Moscow: Muzyka, 1991), 214.

43 See the programs for the 1985 Hamburg Premiere, 58, and for the 2008 Hamburg revival, 7.

44 Irene Hsaio, "Interview with John Neumeier, February 2016," https:// irenechsiao.wordpress.com/2016/02/23/interview-with-john-neumeier-february-2016 (accessed October 1, 2018).

45 See Kremer, *Öbertone*, 132–33; and Wolfgang Willaschek, ed., *Zwanzig Jahre John Neumeier und Das Hamburg Ballett, 1973–1993: Aspekte, Themen, Variationen, Das Zweite Jahrzehnt* (Hamburg: Christians, 1993), 75. The ZDF television broadcast is available in its entirety at the Internationales Theaterinstitut/Mime Centrum Berlin, http://archiv.mimecentrum.de/videos/MCB-DV-3771; and in part (Act 1 through Act 2, Scene 5) at ADK, Archiv Theater der Freien Volksbühne Berlin, AVM 33.3043.

46 Festschrift, 231.

47 From the program book for the Hamburg Ballet performances of *Othello* at Harris Theater, Chicago, February 23 and 24, 2016, 4.

48 Horst Koegler, *John Neumeier: Bilder eines Lebens/Pictures from a Life*, ed. Stiftung John Neumeier (Hamburg: Edel, 2010), 106 (German), 222 (English).

49 Quoted in Willaschek, *Zwanzig Jahre John Neumeier und Das Hamburg Ballett*, 77–78.

50 Ibid., 78.

51 Hsaio, "Interview with John Neumeier."

52 Clips from the ballet are available on YouTube, such as the very affecting Act 1, Scene 3 duet between Desdemona and Othello set to Pärt's *Spiegel im Spiegel*, https://www.youtube.com/watch?v=Jpwz6FLFqBw.

53 Taruskin, *The Oxford History of Western Music*, 5: 415–17.

54 Representative reviews include Eva-Elisabeth Fischer, "Vertanzte Sekundärliteratur: John Neumeiers Othello Ballett in der Hamburger Kampnagelfabrik uraufgeführt," *Stuttgarter Zeitung*, January 29, 1985; and Jochen Schmidt, "Kopf unten, Füße oben: John Neumeiers 'Othello' in der Hamburger Kampnagelfabrik," *Frankfurter Allgemeine Zeitung*, January 29, 1985, 23. These and several of the other reviews cited here can be found at ADK, Sammlung Marna King, 351.

55 ADK, Sammlung Marna King, 351 (original in English, under "Style of Movement").

56 From the *Journal der Hamburgischen Staatsoper*, 1985; quoted in Willaschek, *Zwanzig Jahre John Neumeier und Das Hamburg Ballett*, 78.

57 Monika Fabry and Janos Hörömpö, "Othello führt zu Aggressionen," *Hamburger Abendblatt*, January 26, 1985, A26.

58 Klaus Geitel, "Leiden und leiden lassen," *Die Welt*, January 29, 1985.

59 Kholopova, 120.

60 Sanjoy Roy, "Dracula," *Guardian*, September 6, 2005, https://www.theguardian.com/stage/2005/sep/06/dance; as well as https://boosey.com/pages/cr/calendar/Default?d=11&m=9&y=2014.

## CHAPTER 6

1 See *Critical Edition*, 97. Schnittke had fewer doubts about the accompaniment at the end. A draft of the final string chord can be found on sketch sheet A4:14, where twenty pitches are indicated within the octave from C to C, by half step and, at times, quarter step, to be played as harmonics. The final chord in the published score has twenty pitches, without any harmonics, consisting of half steps and quarter-tones. The C in the bass is duplicated, at several octaves, by the C in cello 3.

2 Nikitina, *Sovetskaia muzyka*, 215–16.

3 Peter J. Schmelz, "'Crucified on the Cross of Mass Culture': Late Soviet Genre Politics in Alexander Zhurbin's Rock Opera *Orpheus and Eurydice*," *Journal of Musicological Research* 28 (2009): 61–87.

4 Nikitina, *Sovetskaia muzyka*, 216.

5 See the treatment of these shots in Vida T. Johnson and Graham Petrie, *The Films of Andrei Tarkovsky: A Visual Fugue* (Bloomington: Indiana University Press, 1994), 145, 152.

6 Ibid., 150.

7 Aldo Tassone, "Interview with Andrei Tarkovsky (on *Stalker*)," in *Andrei Tarkovsky: Interviews*, ed. John Gianvito (Jackson: University Press of Mississippi, 2006), 59.

8 Ibid., 60.

9 Geoff Dyer, *Zona: A Book about a Film about a Journey to a Room* (New York: Pantheon, 2012), 212.

10 Tassone, "Interview with Andrei Tarkovsky," 59.

11 Ibid.

12 *Besedy*, 168 (2005).

13 Vladimir Vysotsky, *O vremeni i o sud'be: Ballady*, Melodiia LP, S40-29415-001 (1990); 30,100 copies were pressed.

14 The specific recording is not identified, but the timing (2:40) and sound most closely match the Kremer and Grindenko 1977 recording (2:56).

15 The exact same moment—the very end of the Rondo—also opens side 2.

16 Vladimir Vysotsky, *Sochineniia v dvukh tomakh* (Yekaterinburg: Posyltorg, 1994), 2: 188.

17 Savenko, "Portret khudozhnika v zrelosti," 38; and Savenko, "V rakurse postmoderna," 547.

18 Tiedman, review of various Schnittke recordings, 48.

19 He possibly meant the 1988–90 Gramzapis' CD pairing of the two compositions (concerto grosso and cello concerto; see appendix).

20 Volker Schlöndorff, "Schlöndorff on Schnittke," liner notes to *Der Neunte Tag/ The Ninth Day, Featuring the Music of Alfred Schnittke*, BIS-CD-1507 (2004); translation amended. This is from a March 21, 2004, radio interview.

21 David Weininger, "At a Dark Season Opener, Compelling Chaos," *Boston Globe*, November 2, 2009. The video can be found at: https://vimeo.com/14901472.

22 A review, originally by P.O. in *Aachener Nachrichten*, was reprinted (with cuts) as "Passionskonzert mit Raritäten," *Das Orchester* 37, nos. 7–8 (1989): 781.

23 Michael Long argues that all classical music today possesses an air of mortality and the macabre; see his *Beautiful Monsters: Imagining the Classic in Musical Media* (Berkeley: University of California Press, 2008), 26 and passim.

24 Marcia Adair, "Naxos Goes Bold with Digital-Only Classical Music Titles," *Los Angeles Times*, October 26, 2011, http://articles.latimes.com/2011/oct/26/entertainment/la-et-digital-compilations-20111026, accessed October 1, 2018.

25 Krysa, interview.

26 Shnitke and Petrov, "Pervaia simfoniia," 44.

27 Lewinski, *Gidon Kremer*, 112; and Schwarz, *Music and Musical Life in Soviet Russia*, 632.

28 See Schmelz, "Selling Schnittke," 426–27, 428.

29 Krysa, interview.

30 Liner notes to Alfred Schnittke, *Concerto Grosso III, Sonata for Violin & Chamber Orchestra, Trio Sonata*, BIS CD, 537 (1991), 3 and 7 (translation amended); Festschrift, 102.

31 Festschrift, 90.

32 Deutsche Grammophon CD, 437 091-2 (1993).

33 See *Critical Edition*, 7.

34 See Schmelz, *Sonic Overload*, for more about these performances and the Violin Concerto no. 4 more generally.

35 Festschrift, 95–96.

36 Ulrike Böhmer, "Beeinflusst durch Schnittke? Eine Umfrage unter Komponisten des deutschsprachigen Raums," in *Postmoderne hinter dem Eisernen Vorhang: Werk und Rezeption Alfred Schnittkes im Kontext ost- und mitteleuropäischer Musikdiskurse*, ed. Amrei Flechsig and Stefan Weiss (Hildesheim: Georg Olms Verlag, 2013), 274.

37 "Prodolzhenie kollektsii 'Velikie kompozitory,'" *Komsomol'skaia pravda*, September 9, 2010, http://www.kp.ru/daily/24555/731080, accessed December 29, 2018.

38 "100 muzykal'nykh sochinenii, s kotorykh nuzhno nachinat' slushat' klassiku," *Afisha-Daily*, December 20, 2015, http://daily.afisha.ru/music/30-100-vazhnejshih-proizvedenij-klassicheskoj-mzyki, accessed January 2, 2019.

39 Joseph Pasternak, dir., *Black Square* (*Chernyi kvadrat*, 1988), *Glasnost Film Festival*, Vol. 7 (Oakland, CA: The Video Project, 2014); translation mine.

40 Quoted in William Quillen, "After the End: New Music in Russia from *Perestroika* to the Present" (Ph.D. diss., University of California, Berkeley, 2010), 102.

41  See https://www.youtube.com/watch?v=ygluZotB8S4, at 2:13:11, accessed January 2, 2019. Schnittke's Polka (an arrangement of a section from the *Gogol Suite*) appeared in the closing ceremonies; see 1:39:00 of https://www.youtube.com/watch?v=FAv9MJm5ylQ&t=8277s.

42  Tim Rutherford-Johnson, *Music after the Fall: Modern Composition and Culture since 1989* (Oakland: University of California Press, 2017), 31, 33, 75; and Schmelz, "Selling Schnittke," 438–39.

43  Friederike Wißmann, *Deutsche Musik* (Munich: Piper, 2017). She briefly discusses Pärt on 62.

44  *Reader*, 169.

45  Sophie Fiennes, Slavoj Žižek, et al., *Pervert's Guide to Cinema*, Part 3, Chapters 20 and 21 (DVD, Mischief Films and Microcinema, 2006).

46  Tracey K. Smith, "My God, It's Full of Stars," from *Life on Mars: Poems* (Minneapolis: Graywolf Press, 2011), 10.

47  Svetlana Savenko, "Pominki po sovetskoi opere," *Iskusstvo kino*, no. 12 (December 1993): 53.

48  Sokolov, *Muzykal'naia kompozitsiia XX veka*, 65.

49  Krysa, interview.

# INDEX